# DOING
# BUSINESS
# GOD'S
# WAY

Other books by Dennis Peacocke:

*On the Destiny of Nations*

*Winning the Battle for the Minds of Men*

*The Emperor Has No Clothes*

# DOING BUSINESS GOD'S WAY

## Dennis Peacocke

# Doing Business God's Way

## DENNIS PEACOCKE

Originally published as
*Doing Business God's Way, Almighty & Sons,* © 1995

Published by REBUILD
P.O. Box 2492
Santa Rosa, California 95405

Revised and expanded
© 2003 by Dennis Peacocke

Second edition 2014

ISBN 978-1-887021-03-6

*Printed and bound in the United States of America*

To my father,
Fred Peacocke,
whose love of history
and profound interest
in man's running
of the world
helped make of him
an ethical businessman
and a lover of God's Earth

Many people have helped me
with the writing of this book.
The First Edition,
some eight years and countless
teaching sessions back,
was only possible because of numerous
people's generous assistance.
With this third major printing,
it is also true that nothing of significance
is done alone or without many helping hands.
Thank you, my friends;
it appears that our common labor
is making some measure of difference.

# CONTENTS

ix   *Preface*

xi   *Introduction:*     Economic Evangelism: Catching the
Fish with Their Own Food

## Section One

### God's Essential Principles for Building Government and Free Enterprise

1   *Chapter One:*     **God Is Building a Family Business
MASTER PRINCIPLE #1:**
God is the Creator of private property.

17   *Chapter Two:*     **Maturity Comes by Stewarding Property
MASTER PRINCIPLE #2:**
We grow by caring for people and things.

31   *Chapter Three:*     **Generational Wealth and the Family Unit
MASTER PRINCIPLE #3:**
All lasting wealth comes through the
family unit and is built generationally.

49   *Chapter Four:*     **Our God Loves to Work
MASTER PRINCIPLE #4:**
Work is a holy, everlasting calling.

61   *Chapter Five:*     **The Product of the Family Business
Is Service
MASTER PRINCIPLE #5:**
Service is the foundation
of all lasting growth.

# Section Two

## The Foundations Required to Build a Prosperous and Just Society

75 *Chapter Six:* **What Money Reveals about People**
**MASTER PRINCIPLE #6:**
God pays for what He orders.

89 *Chapter Seven:* **Risk, Self-Respect, and Redemptive Struggle**
**MASTER PRINCIPLE #7:**
The possibility of a failure is essential for human growth.

103 *Chapter Eight:* **Exposing the Cruelty of the Economics of Blame**
**MASTER PRINCIPLE #8:**
Ideas and actions have economic consequences.

119 *Chapter Nine:* **Justice and Equality Are Not the Same**
**MASTER PRINCIPLE #9:**
Men are not equal, and economic redistribution cannot change this fact.

131 *Chapter Ten:* **Godly Government Produces Peace and Productivity**
**MASTER PRINCIPLE #10:**
Functioning biblical government is essential for productivity.

143 *Chapter Eleven:* **The Essential Threefold Cords that Will Lead to Your Success**
**MASTER PRINCIPLE #11:**
Christians must live as disciples, renew their minds, and come together in unity to execute God's plan for the nations.

153 *Chapter Twelve:* **A Call to True Radicals**
**MASTER PRINCIPLE #12:**
Discover the root structures and build out from them.

# Preface

*T*his book was the result of years of study, conversations, and seminars which I taught on the general content in the 1980s. What has always seemed clear to me is that "spiritual truth" that does not result in measurable change in the here-and-now is either not yet clearly understood or irrelevant. For sure, economics and business are about here-and-now reality, and the issue therefore is to connect these endeavors and ground them to their spiritual foundations in the God who created them.

The purpose of this book is threefold. Firstly, it is to acknowledge God as the author and upholder of all concepts and practices related to stewardship, creation of resources, social justice, and successful organization-building. Secondly, it is to help reposition the way many Christians think about God's purposes for humanity and the manner in which God's own revealed actions model for us where He wants to take us. Thirdly, it is to help undergird and facilitate the rapidly emerging interest in marketplace ministry, and its validity to God, for countless millions of believers.

Over time, I have also observed that numbers of business people have struggled deeply with the role of the local church in their lives and marketplace ministries. While many pastors have become preoccupied with their own ecclesiastic roles and vision, tending to ignore other valid ministries not directly related to running a church, growing numbers of church leaders have given very specific value and recognition to marketplace ministries and other essential outward Kingdom ministry into the community. The New Testament is clear by emphasis that the local church is non-negotiably important to the grounding and development of believers. I am very grateful for the pastors and business ministries that believe this and are partnering to make a difference, both within the church and as it reaches out into the world around it to bring transformation.

Today we face many crises. None of them is more basic than the answer to this question: How should mankind justly care for the Earth's resources and distribute its wealth? If Christianity really is God's message to the world, and the Bible is His "manufacturer's handbook," then scripture must address this most fundamental question of human concern. Has our Maker established laws governing our labor, our currencies, our productive justice, and other general laws related to what we commonly call "economics"? If so, how do they work? Does the Bible address those laws? What are the penalties for individuals, businesses, and nations breaking those laws? This became the basis of my original search and my subsequent teaching. The answers to these questions are in this book.

As might be expected, Jesus said it most clearly: "...for where your treasure is, there will your heart be also."[1] If you find my treasure, you find my heart. This is the most basic of all truths and the foundation of all studies of human nature. The study of hearts and treasures is all about economics and all about business. Christianity is, indeed, about the study of man at his most basic level and the God who made him so.

Whoever produces both capital and human justice will lead the 21st century. This book establishes a biblical foundation which I believe can both help in that cause and undergird a compassionate, free-enterprise system that is truly based upon Christ's Kingdom. The whole of mankind desperately needs you and me to give ourselves to this cause. The church stands at the threshold of an enormous possibility for both relevance and global leadership. May we respond to that challenge as men and women who are living lives that are centered beyond our own self-serving interests.

Finally, upon reflection, this book is designed to be "evangelistic." By that I mean it introduces an eminently practical and empowering Being to those who may have been looking for Him in the clouds instead of having feet squarely planted in the practices of men's lives. Welcome to the "franchise of all time" and those who serve its genius Inventor!

---

[1] Matt. 6:21

# Introduction

## Economic Evangelism: Catching the Fish with Their Own Food

*"And He said to them, 'Follow Me, and I will make you fishers of men.'"*

Matt.4:19

This book is built upon twelve foundational concepts of economic, social, and organizational laws. I have been teaching these twelve concepts and refining them for over twenty years. They address core issues within God's heart and the human heart as well. They are systematically presented for the sake of a progressive and logical presentation, but not necessarily in order of importance. What I will say about them is this: These concepts are grounded in scriptural truth and, therefore, correctly applied, they work. Indeed, truth never fails.

God's plan to change the world is Himself. He has created the world, and He will change it primarily through His people, who are commonly called "the Church." The word *Church* comes from the Greek word "ekklesia," which literally means those elected and called out to rule. Those of you familiar with Greek history know about the role of ekklesia in ancient Greek politics within the city-states. They were the rulers and the business managers of their culture. The Church is supposed to be an army of rulers, hence the Holy Spirit chose the word "ekklesia" to describe her. This is no small truth.

Rulership has always been connected with managerial responsibilities. How can a man rule in the ekklesia (church) of God if he isn't a good ruler in his own home over his family?[1] Before you establish the rules and a plan for how things are designed to operate most effectively and efficiently, you need rulership. Is God a ruler? Obviously! Does He have a plan by which mankind and nations operate most effectively and efficiently? Yes, yes, and yes!

---

[1] 1 Tim. 3:4; Gen. 18:18

He has a plan called His "gospel"; a detailed blueprint of it called the "Bible"; a work force designed to implement His plan called His "Church"; and a C.E.O. called the Holy Spirit who is everywhere at once. What a potential operation! The major problem is the work force—the believers. They don't understand the work project because they have focused on their retirement benefits in the future and in Heaven. Clearly they should focus on the work project God has given them to do on Earth.

Alas, God's employees have been told by many of their leaders that what really counts is the retirement village in Heaven and not the passion and challenge of contributing to His enterprise here on Earth. Let me ask those of you who manage or hire people what you would think about the character and motivation of a prospective employee whose primary focus was on the benefits and retirement plans of your organization. Would you really want to hire such a self-oriented person? Can you now see why so much of Christendom is in such an apathetic mess? We've focused on the retirement plan and therefore have attracted self-interested people. The go-getters in the world look down their noses at us. The corporations snatch up the very kind of people Christ says belong to His Kingdom enterprise, namely, the "violent men" who "take it (the Kingdom) by force."[2]

God not only has a business plan, but He has extended it out into the ages to come and preplanned each step before He created His worlds.[3] His children shall be working with Him forever. He is not in a hurry because His primary product is the quality of life and maturity that His employees and co-workers are experiencing with Him as He is extending the influence of His business (Kingdom). This is a major principle and one that you and I, as apprentices, are expected to understand, practice, and master. God's business plan is designed to produce proprietorship and maturity in His business partners. Any family, business, church, or nation that builds on this principle will be blessed by God and prosper since He is into blessing people who run their businesses the way He runs His. But we are getting ahead

---

[2] Matt. 11:12b
[3] Rev. 13:8

of ourselves, and right now we need to refocus on God's overall business plan.

Jesus was amazed that His earthly family guardians, Mary and Joseph, were full of anxiety concerning His whereabouts. Parenthetically, how would you like to have been responsible for losing God? Talk about poor stewardship! His response to them when they found Him in the temple conversing with the leaders, was a classic: "Wist ye not that I must be about my Father's business?" [4] Frankly, Jesus, no! We didn't know your Father had a business or that you could possibly frame your work in such a down-to-earth and possibly even carnal way so as to talk about God as a business person.

Now, while you may be thinking that it is a "stretch" to apply Christ's quote about Father's "business" here to real-life business, please remember this: Business is about an exchange of values between two or more parties. In this sense, the gospel is "business." Is this "business orientation" talk of Jesus inconsistent with the rest of His message? Hardly. Consider this, please: There are more parables concerning the stewardship of material goods and personal talents in the New Testament than concern Heaven or any other single topic. God is not only materially oriented; He invented all matter and owns it all to boot. He has an earthly business franchise. He intends to return someday in person and then extend His employee/ joint owners' influence into the rulership and management of all that He has created. [5] He has an evil unrelenting competitor named Satan whose rival operation has seized much of the Earth. Satan has been largely unchallenged by most believers because they thought the retirement plan was the issue, not the earthly franchise. And to make it all the more practical, both Satan and God are competing for the market share of the people who make up Earth's population. The undecided and the ignorant are evangelism's goal. God created them and, as a loving Steward, wants them functioning as He intended.

So how should we go about "fishing" for them on God's behalf? After all, Jesus said that He would make us "fishers of men." [6] What are

---

[4] Luke 2:49 (KJV)
[5] Rom. 8:17; Eph. 1
[6] Matt. 4:19

the fish feeding on? They aren't biting much on retirement plans, I'll tell you that for sure. No, they're feeding on the practical issues of life such as these:

- How can I best provide for myself and my family?
- How can I live in safety and protect myself, my family, and my property from violence, theft, confiscation, and social collapse?
- How can I make and maintain real, meaningful relationships?
- How can the system I live in provide security, justice and economic opportunity?

These are the kinds of questions people all over the Earth are asking and precisely the kinds of questions we Christians are not answering. We are refusing to look away from the future retirement plan of our gospel to be able to deal with these here-and-now questions. They seem too carnal and earthly. However, if we truly care for people (the fish), why do we insist that they eat what *we* want to feed them, instead of giving them the things for which they hunger? Christians are the only fishermen I know who demand that the fish change their feeding habits, come to the sporting goods store (our church), and voluntarily put the hooks in their own mouths! Here is my point: The nations are looking for people with a plan for how to live successfully here on this Earth. The issue is not on what *should* the unsaved be feeding, but rather, on what *are* they feeding.

The three most important issues in U.S. Presidential elections are consistently these: economics, economics, and economics. Where people's treasure is, there will their hearts be also. This preoccupation with the practical is not all bad since God and His gospel are immensely practical. What's truly unfortunate are Christians who live in the real world, but refuse to deal with the real issues in it. This is tragic because it misrepresents God and because it allows the evil world system to exploit people and take away their ability to fully experience freedom, growth, and productivity from God's point of view. And it is likewise unacceptable because it shrouds the retirement plan in future promises, rather than in God's demonstrated effectiveness in the here-and-now business of this life. If God's gospel doesn't work now, here on Earth, why should we expect unbelievers to trust in it for a future richness of life in Heaven?

But, God's business plan will unfold as His people begin to see how serious He really is. He's in the business of overcoming the competition, closing the deal on the uncommitted fish, and demonstrating the obvious superiority of His principles of life in the one realm which preoccupies the whole world: the just provision for our lives (economics).

I believe economic evangelism is the next major wave of the future for a number of reasons:

1) Economic issues are a universal bait of all people.

2) The gospel clearly explains how to follow the manufacturer's (God's) purposes for people and His uses for the created order.

3) God's laws of personal and corporate freedom, dignity, growth, and justice operate perfectly in a self-rewarding and competitive environment.

4) Business and financial success are both easily measured. Hence, unlike politics, social justice, etc., business people can apply God's Word and then personally see that it works without undue complicating factors.

5) Christians have access to God's wisdom to deal with all of the above, and we are operating in a *massive seller's market of desperate human need.*

What a dynamite situation! All we have to do now is better understand Father's business plan and put it into operation in our own lives and places of responsibility.

*Doing Business God's Way* is an introductory study to the master principles of management, growth, and productivity that God has revealed in His Word. May we see and practice these principles. The nations are waiting for us as they flounder in the grip of tyranny, confusion, and systems of economic mismanagement that can only fail and oppress them.

## Our Journey Together—We Must Change as Individuals before We Change the Culture

This book is divided into two sections. *Section One* deals with the theological issues affecting the individual believer and his or her role in the marketplace, and *Section Two* takes those same issues and principles and shows how they, of necessity, must affect the political world in which we live. We move from the private to the public.

If truth doesn't work at home it isn't truth. If truth doesn't work in the marketplace, it won't work in Congress or the courts either because something is fundamentally wrong with it. Stated positively, if principles work at home and in the marketplace, they will work equally well in governing a nation with order, justice and productivity.

*Section One* attempts to explain how a clear understanding of God's vision for His children and their work radically changes our personal lives and releases us into a whole new world of creativity and freedom.

*Section Two* assumes two things: (1) we're losing our current freedom because we're rejecting even the historic truths we did have, and (2) you and I want to reverse this slide into chaos and economic bondage by practicing God's truths in the marketplace and electing leaders who will do so in our public institutions. Both issues lie squarely at the feet of Christians. Indeed, believers are to be Almighty's mouth, hands, and feet on this Earth, for they are stationed here to operate His earthly franchise, and to empower people and deliver them from ignorance and bondage.

# God's Essential Principles for Building Government and Free Enterprise

# Chapter One

# God Is Building a Family Business

*"...wist ye not that I must be about my Father's business?"*　　　Luke 2:49 (KJV)

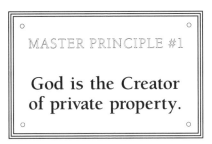

MASTER PRINCIPLE #1

**God is the Creator of private property.**

What is God doing on the Earth today? What has He been doing from the beginning? What can we expect from Him tomorrow and for the many years that will come and go before He brings history to its end? All too often the answer is that He's frantically working to save a bunch of people before the end, or before they die, so that He can populate Heaven. But if that were so, God could have dispensed with the majority of scripture, which addresses our responsibilities here on Earth, and cut straight to the retirement plan waiting for us in the future.

We could say that God is building His Kingdom. That would be true. But that answer would also be likely to fall on deaf ears, because too many Christians have heard about "the Kingdom of God" for so long that they no longer pay attention to it. The phrase has lost much of its substance from overuse, misuse, and abuse.

Instead, I like to say that God is a businessman, and He's building a business. Novel as this language may seem, it is biblical. Grasping it can revolutionize how we understand our role in history, as we saw in the introduction.

The prevailing lifestyle in much of the evangelical world reveals an attitude of, "We've got our salvation, and since God controls history, let's just take care of our own personal affairs, avoid major sin, witness when possible, build 'successful churches,' and then get out of here."

That isn't what God wants. In Genesis 1:26-28, God states that we are created in His image and likeness to have dominion over the

Earth and everything in it. That means we are created to have the same intrinsic goals, desires, and ambitions as God, and that they are to be realized first of all on Earth before we graduate into the future. God intends to bring life on Earth under His order, and He intends to use believers to do it. This is why we are to "seek first the Kingdom"[1] and to pray, "Thy Kingdom come, Thy will be done, on Earth as it is in heaven."[2] Heaven has no problems; the work is here on Earth.

### God Wants to Extend "Almighty & Sons" to the Earth through Us

Let's say it simply: God the Father is building a family business. I call it ALMIGHTY & SONS. He wants each of His children to have a franchise in that business. He wants the business to grow through each of us. God wants to bring His own brand of *McDonald's* down to Earth and give every believer a piece of the action. Through each local franchise, He wants His children to reap its blessings, and He wants the needy, hurting people of the world to benefit from the services His business offers. A franchise does that. It supplies the expertise and power, and you supply the local outlet.

When you were born again, you were born into the family. You became a joint heir with Christ in the enterprise.[3] From that moment, Father began grooming you to take your place in the family business alongside all the other family members. Why do we refer to God's work in the world as the family business? Because that is how Christ speaks in the Parable of the Minas.[4] A nobleman, who represents Christ Himself, distributes to each of his servants one mina (about three months' salary) before leaving on a long trip and says to them, "Do business (literally: trade) until I come" (verse 13). When he returns, he calls each of them to him "that he might know how much every man had gained by trading," (literally: by conducting business)(verse 15). Having accounted for their gains, he gives them

---

[1] Matt. 6:33
[2] Matt. 6:10
[3] Rom. 8:17
[4] Luke 19:11-27 (KJV)

new responsibilities proportionate to their proven business acumen. The parable of the minas depicts how Christ rules over His Kingdom and apportions work, the sort of work associated with running a business, to His servant children.

If you are in Christ, you are called to extend His Kingdom franchise on Earth as a junior partner.[5] You are called to discover His management principles of life, relationships, and stewardship in the scriptures; practice them personally and with others; and let the Holy Spirit train you as to their proper use and appropriate applications. You are to become a "company man" or a "company woman." Like Jesus, you are to seek every possible opportunity to extend Father's life and blessings to all men and all situations. You are also called to apply godly stewardship and care over the resources entrusted to you and to root out the enemy/competitor (Satan) from your own life and your family. You're to look for opportunities to attack Hell's gates[6] and liberate those whose minds, morals, and lifestyles have been imprisoned by Satan's world system. You didn't just get saved, you got drafted! You're in His family business to extend it both within you and externally to the uttermost parts of the Earth. It runs on laws which you are expected to learn and apply in an ever-increasing masterly fashion. You, friend, are in God's M.B.A. program, and the only issue is what kind of student/ employee you are. Are you looking out for yourself and your retirement program in the sky, or are you looking out for the extension of Father's business affairs here on Earth like Jesus did?

This book is set up around Twelve Master Principles of biblical economics and management. Each of the Twelve Master Principles have direct corollaries, or spin-off truths, that touch major areas of management and also national and international economic issues as well. The master principle which we will discuss here in chapter one deals with God's creation of private property. It is "square one" in terms of the whole study, and forms what I believe is the introduction to any biblical study on economics.

---

[5] Rom. 8:17
[6] Matt. 16:18

## If Owning Things Is a Sin, God Is the Chief of Sinners

God is the author of the concept that is called "private property." He created all things, both spiritual and material, and owns them all. If you have fallen for the anti-biblical, gnostic heresy that owning material things is unspiritual and carnal, then you must logically believe that God is the chief of sinners and the most carnal of us all. But I doubt if you really believe that. It is only what false teachers have tried to teach us. Hopefully, they didn't understand the implications of their own false teaching. What is true is that private, material property, and all the biblical rights and responsibilities surrounding it, is *God's idea,* not carnal exploitative man's or Satan's. God declares Himself the only true and rightful property owner of all material things: "The Earth is the Lord's, and all it contains, the world, and those who dwell in it."[7]

Obviously this does not mean that material ownership should lead to crass indifference, ignoring the genuine material needs of others. Anyone who knows about the kinds of community service projects I encourage and facilitate knows better. But let's set the record straight from God's Word: All resources are owned by God and on loan to man to steward for Him. They are to be used to generally further God's Kingdom franchise on Earth. Rousseau, Karl Marx, or any left-wing professor who attacks the concept of private property, and who knows anything about its origin, are simply anti-Christ in their false assertion that all private property is theft.

Without going into a philosophy lesson, this anti-property and anti-material garbage is actually a very old form of what is called "gnostic philosophy" and was resolutely fought against for hundreds of years by the early church fathers. It is called "dualism" and essentially says that spirit is "good" and matter is "evil"; and that to become truly spiritual one must reject all material things and live in "the spirit." Of course, the Holy Spirit exhorts us to be fully blessed and prosper in every way,[8] that is, both in spiritual and in natural things.

---

[7] Psa. 24:1
[8] 3 John verse 2

## God Is after Incarnating Truth
## Rather Than Calling Us All to Poverty

Christianity, and the whole world, have been catastrophically affected by two things: first, the belief that true spirituality can primarily only exist in poverty; and second, that true spirituality must reject the material world and the challenges in it. I would like to remind us all of the two major truths directly related to this attack against the material world, and owning or managing things, services, etc.

1. As Paul tells us in Philippians, chapter two, Jesus "emptied Himself" of all that He owned in order to please the Father and demonstrate humility. He gave up His heavenly power out of virtue, not because what He owned was inherently evil. If it was evil, why did He ask for all of it back in John 17:5? He triumphed over all things by emptying Himself of His inherent right to them as their Creator. This principle of "moving in the opposite spirit" is very deep and beyond our study here. The point is this: Jesus became poor for a season and for a reason. Upon completion of His first advent, He was once again clothed in all the majesty, power, and ownership He had ever possessed. [9]

2. Rather than rejecting the material world and the management of it, God ordains it. God incarnates His spiritual ideas *into* the material world. Jesus Christ is "Exhibit A": "The Word became flesh and dwelt among us." [10] When God has an idea, He incarnates it into His Cosmos. He operates directly opposite to the false teachers who want to get everything *out of matter,* into the spirit. God is moving to get His Spirit controlling His believers so that they will bring His creation into His order.

---

[9] John 17:5
[10] John 1:14

I clearly remember one day in 1987 when I was out jogging, and God's Spirit impressed me with the statement: "Dennis, you and I are going in opposite directions. I'm moving more and more to get *on* the Earth, and you're waiting to get off it." I began to weep, for I began to comprehend the problem. God's kids are trying to get off the planet and into the "spirit," while God is moving to get increasingly *on* the planet and *into* the material world through His children, to extend His franchise. All of a sudden Christ's prayer, "Thy kingdom come, thy will be done, on Earth as it is in heaven" (Matt. 6:10), took on a whole new level of understanding. The problems aren't in the spirit in Heaven, but rather in the material world here on Earth! This is where the action is, and the franchise is to be extended. No wonder Satan wants us to reject the material world and the stewardship and management of it. He wants it for himself and *his* franchise. It's a smart move, but not smart enough. God's kids are waking up, and those who are engifted with management skill and understanding are especially aroused. They know that their product is substantially superior to Satan's.

## In God's Kingdom, There Are No Second-Class Citizens

The false teaching against material stewardship has had especially devastating results against the average Christian, who, unlike the pastor, is called to earn his living dealing with the material world. It has promoted a kind of "second-class citizenship" in the Church. If you're spiritual, or "called to the ministry," you go full-time into God's work. If not, you work in the fallen world, contribute where you can, and sometimes wonder why God didn't love you enough to let you be "full-time" and out from under the burden of the material world. At best you may become a deacon or Sunday school teacher, but you feel tainted by material things. At worst you become a "cash cow" to the local church and are called upon to keep its projects running in the black.

Praise God, there is a spiritual revolution in the making, one like unto Martin Luther's "priesthood of all believers" revolution. Not only are all believers priests before the Lord, [11] as Luther maintained, but

---

[11] 1 Peter 2:9

all Spirit-directed vocations are ordained by God and intrinsically of value. God's Kingdom franchise requires workers of all kinds: plumbers, C.P.A.'s, salesmen, housewives, and corporate executives. All of them are called to extend Father's will and the ways of His Kingdom into every sphere of life. You are no longer a second-class citizen, once you see God as the Property Owner and the spirit-made-flesh Material Manager. We should have had a clue to this liberating truth the first time we read Exodus 31:1-3, where the first "Spirit-filled" people in Moses' congregation were artisans and craftsmen.

As a pastor and businessman, I can honestly say that if many businesses were run like many churches are run, they would be broke in a year. That isn't a slam against pastors or churches as much as it is a statement of our universal stupidity in the Church. In trying so hard to be "spiritual" we have often rejected the obvious biblical skills associated with planning, strategic objectives, budget analysis, productivity, accountability, and many other "worldly" management skills—simply because we thought they only operated in the world of property, not the world of souls. Thankfully we see that kind of gnostic nonsense beginning to yield to God, the Property Owner, and God, the Strategic Thinker. The franchise is beginning to be seen, and it is mostly business professionals and everyday saints who are responding. Managing people and things isn't a sin; it's a franchise mandate.

## Our Time on Earth Develops Our Spiritual Skills

In Galatians 3:23 to 4:7, Paul magnificently points out that God's children are kept under tutors, trained and prepared by those tutors, until the Father calls them to Himself for more managerial responsibility. Under the disciplines of Earth life, God will someday call us fully to Himself, not as slaves, but as heirs.[12] Having been trained during our earthly visit to deal with life, reality, relational challenges, and material management problems, we will be ready for more training and responsibility. Fruitful saints will rule over cities, not harps, in the next age. Some will even rule over whole nations[13] rather than golden

---

[12] Gal. 4:7
[13] Matt. 24:46-47; Luke 12:44; Rev. 2:26

slippers. For God is the Ultimate Manager of His Cosmos, and He is training up His kids to rule it all under Christ, using planet Earth as square one. Indeed, since power is guarded by problems, all the franchise trainees will get ample opportunity to learn how to apply God's Word toward solving problems here on Earth.

Earth is our workshop assigned by God, and we are not here simply to keep ourselves from sin. We are also here to drive sin away and nullify its effect in the created order.

In Matthew 16:18, Jesus says the gates of Hell will not prevail against His Church. Most Christians live as if our job were to keep the gates of Hell from swallowing us up until, at the last minute, Jesus rescues us. That is not Christ's point.

Jesus calls us the "ekklesia." The ekklesia was an institution familiar for centuries throughout the Hellenic world. It was the representative assembly that ruled over civic affairs. It was not a ragtag guerrilla army or a cowering, persecuted minority; it was the duly constituted authority. By calling His people the ekklesia (which we translate "church"), Christ implicitly gives us authority in world affairs. That is part of why the Roman Empire considered the Church such a challenge and was so threatened by it.

Christ's intent is not that we should bar the gates and somehow weather Hell's fury; it is that we, acting under His authority as His ekklesia, should storm the gates of Hell and crush them, radically reducing Hell's influence in the world and so expressing the truth that Christ is all in all.

## Most of Our Trials Are Lessons to Be Learned

Earth is our workshop, and it is filled with trials, challenges, and opposition, all of which are intended by God for our growth. We are to attack Hell's gates. We are on the offensive, and our weapons are not guns and bombs. They are obedience to God's Word, prayer, preaching, teaching, debate, and self-sacrificial service to those in need. With these we cast down false spiritual ideologies and practices that enslave people. In short, we discover and practice a biblical worldview, a way of seeing and practicing God's reality and decrees for His Earth. When, by the Holy Spirit, we put God's Word into practice through this biblical worldview, revival will naturally follow.

In Father's workshop, we are being prepared for Heaven. But most believers don't want to deal with the problems God serves up in the workshop. They assume that all their troubles are Satan's attacks. Indeed, I am convinced that if Satan didn't exist, believers would invent him! Most of our challenges are exercises, lessons God has prepared for us in the workshop. If we would stop ascribing them to the devil and start receiving them as lessons from God to be solved with His Word, we would experience the power of God's Word in a whole new practical way. Then we would be like "those who by reason of use (that is, practice) have their senses exercised to discern both good and evil." [14]

All of these truths relate back to God's creation of the material world, His command for man to steward it on His behalf, and to solve problems God's way. The reason we must spend so much time in this chapter on these theological foundations is that without this foundation you will constantly be in danger of falling off one side of the road or the other. On the one side, we fall into simple materialism, forgetting that the issue is stewarding God's resources with God's purposes and methods rather than "getting rich." On the other side is the ditch of false spirituality which rejects the management of property and resources in favor of "full time ministry" or "spiritual" things. Balanced ministry seeks neither goods nor ghosts, but rather God.

## Ruling over Real Things in the Real World Is the Real Issue

As we have already noted, the reason satanic strategy attacks the stewardship of property and material things is so that Satan can rule over the resources of this Earth, and so that the captive nations will be unchallenged by Christianity. Satan believes in his total monopoly. If the kingdoms of both Satan and God require material human bodies

---

[14] Heb. 5:14 (KJV)

and material resources to extend their power (and they both do), then blinding God's people with false and misleading "spiritual" assumptions is essential. Add to this fact the undisputed reality that the vast majority of human beings are preoccupied with how to live successfully in *this* material world, rather than in a future "spiritual" one, and you can quickly see the massive problem we face in light of this truth. Many believers think the gospel of Christ applies primarily to the *future*; hence the gospel becomes less relevant to here-and-now unbelievers. Believers and non-believers aren't even communicating. This message, Christ's Kingdom message, bridges the gap. It clearly shows how today and eternity are linked by the principles of apprenticeship in the here-and-now. Ruling well over what you have now, becomes the stepping stone into your future and the levels of responsibility you will carry.

## Let's Apply What We Learn

The heart of my message is not "save the United States" or any other nation. We're not here to "save" the nations, as much as we may love them, but rather to present ourselves to Father for training in obedience while in His earthly workshop. As we become effective in our obedience, the discipling of the nations will naturally flow from this. We want to become effective tools Father can use to fulfill Christ's destiny, that He should be all in all. We are calling the Church back to the workshop and saying, "Father is building ALMIGHTY & SONS, and in building ALMIGHTY & SONS, He requires us to apply the Book to the whole of human living."

God has given us a tremendous opportunity. Satan's world-system franchise is steering the ship onto the rocks. When the ship hits, it will begin to break up and sink. We can show the world how to get the ship off the rocks and repair it. But to do that, we must stand fast on the truths of scripture and destroy the falsehoods that dominate the world's thinking and have led the world to its present debacle.

Many of us were unaware until the last decade that Jesus meant it when He said, "Occupy (literally: conduct business) until I come" (Luke 19:13 KJV). We thought the name of the game was "get saved, stay holy, stay in your comfortable fellowship, let the world go to Hell," and "Praise God, Jesus is coming to rescue us from this mess that Father can't straighten out." I call that "faith" simple unbelief!

This defeatist message is not the historic gospel. It grew out of eighteenth and nineteenth century secularist "enlightenment" philosophy, and it is the root of the idolatrous notion that Christianity has no solutions to man's temporal problems and is not responsible to lead or care for the Earth and its people. It leads many contemporary evangelicals to think the Bible is fine for telling you how to get to Heaven but says little about how to manage your household, less about how to run a business, and nothing at all about how to govern a city or a nation.

Often this deceit comes clothed in innocent sounding language: "The Bible isn't a textbook on economics" (or science, or law, or government, or anything else but salvation). True enough. It isn't a textbook on any one of these things. It's a textbook *on all of them* and everything else in life, and it doesn't read like a textbook, systematically treating each subject in isolation, because it was inspired by a God who made all of life interwoven so that everything affects everything else.

## A Quick Look at Father's Franchise Building Rules

We won't change the world in the world's way. We won't copy the strategy of the Marxist revolutionaries, or the lords of capitalism, or any other secular movement. Instead, we will build on four biblical principles:

1. Change must work from the inside out, both personally and institutionally.

2. Change must progress from local, to national, to international (i.e., from the bottom up).

3. Change must be comprehensive, affecting every aspect of life, looking from today on into eternity.

4. Change must be affected by the godly stewardship of servant-leaders, not by tyrannical takeovers.

We must build according to God's pattern. God changes the world from the inside out, starts small and grows big, transforms every aspect of life, and uses people with servants' hearts. You do not change a nation for the good by naked legislation. You change it by regeneration and sanctification that bear fruit in changed legislation.

The first two principles, which are closely related to each other, appear in Jesus' statements about the Kingdom: "The Kingdom of God," He said, "cometh not with observation; neither shall they say, 'Lo here!' or 'Lo there!' for, behold, the Kingdom of God is within you."[15]

> What is the Kingdom of God like? And to what shall I compare it? It is like a mustard seed, which a man took and put in his garden; and it grew and became a large tree, and the birds of the air nested in its branches...It is like leaven, which a woman took and hid in three measures of meal until it was all leavened. *Luke 13:18-19, 21*

Not that we don't press for external change. We do. But our confidence is not in changing public policy, whether local or national. It is in the transforming power of God working first in individuals and families, then in wider circles. "Except a man be born again..."[16] This means that there has to be a fundamental regeneration of the human being.

The third principle is that we must build comprehensively. Paul told Timothy that God had put into scripture everything necessary to equip anyone fully "for every good work."[17] Too often we "New Testament Christians" read that in terms of the New Testament alone. But Paul was talking about the Old Testament, because there was no New Testament; it wasn't completed yet. Every admonition in the New Testament to study the scriptures applies directly to the Old Testament and only indirectly to the New. The challenge we face is to study the whole Book with such clarity, anointing, and intensity that we can address all of rebellious man's problems. We need the whole sword, not just the New Testament half!

---

[15] Luke 17:20,21 (KJV)
[16] John 3:3 (KJV)
[17] 2 Tim. 3:16-17

The keys to rebuilding the family are in the Book. The keys to rebuilding the individual are in the Book. The solution to the drug problem is in the Book. The solution to educational failure is in the Book. Difficulties in taxation, agriculture, the environment—the whole onslaught of problems rebellious man has created are to be solved by studying and applying God's Word systematically and strategically. When we take God's Book seriously, God will demonstrate to principalities and powers and all the heavenly onlookers, that great cloud of witnesses, that HIS WORD TRULY IS ALIVE AND POWERFUL AND ABLE TO SOLVE PROBLEMS. DO YOU BELIEVE THAT?

The saints are called to inherit the Earth.[18] We inherit responsibility; not harps, not golden slippers, and not a trip to the eternal retirement village in the great by-and-by. We are called to work because Christ works, and God is committed to work. Remember, work was commissioned before the Fall.[19] Christianity must revitalize the work ethic.

The fourth principle is that true leadership comes through servanthood. Christ said, "...whoever wishes to be first among you shall be your slave; just as the Son of Man did not come to be served, but to serve..." [20] God honors those who, imitating Jesus, humble themselves and take on the form of a bondservant. [21]

We intend to affect social and economic change one step at a time by applying these five corollary truths:

1.   Freedom begins with self-government under God.

2.   The family unit is the basic building block of a healthy community.

3.   The local church is the primary equipping center for effective Christian service.

---

[18] Matt. 5:5
[19] Gen. 1:26-28
[20] Matt. 20:27-28
[21] Phil. 2:5-11

4.  Stewardship of private property is essential to personal and societal maturity.

5.  Rebuilding a nation begins with rebuilding a local community.

We will explore these truths further in the rest of this book. For now, suffice it to say that Jesus Christ brings us to maturity by giving us relationships, talents, and things for which to care.

It is no accident that the socialist agenda, aimed at making people dependent on the idol of the state, has always been: (a) to commandeer public education and snatch the kids; (b) to essentially abolish private property, and to strip the general population of stewardship; and (c) to exterminate the Church or reduce it to a people only dealing with heavenly issues. Those are the three foundations of the new social order: kids, property, and Church. By the way, if you think that the collapse of communist governments means Marxist thinking is no longer a threat, you haven't observed the people and ideas controlling many American universities.

### Economic Upheaval Is the Church's Wake-Up Call

Why emphasize the *private sector*? Because God in His holiness is judging this nation as well as others. His judgment will bring major economic upheaval. God has always used economic judgment in history. Anyone who studies the demise of cultures can see that.

As He progressively de-funds this culture's civil institutions, the private sector will have to emerge to fill the void. The public sector increasingly lacks the revenue to meet people's needs and is going broke. City, state, and federal deficits are rising. The public sector will inevitably turn to the private sector for help. That will be the opportunity for God's people to reclaim a nation through servant-hood and the biblical truths of management which we have learned to practice. It's an opportunity we dare not miss and will not miss, God helping us. The extension of Father's franchise is at stake!

When the wheels come off, we must be ready. Christian businesswoman and businessman: You are at the heart of God's answer to the need. But we can't help fix what we haven't learned how to make work in our own private worlds. This is the work to which we must give ourselves: learning to apply God's Word practically to our sphere of influence. Then the wake-up call will excite us rather than frighten us.

# CHAPTER TWO

# Maturity Comes by Stewarding Property

*"For we must all appear before the judgment seat of Christ, that each one may be recompensed for his deeds in the body..."*                    2 Cor. 5:10

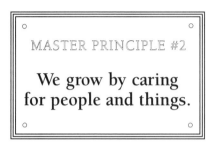

MASTER PRINCIPLE #2

**We grow by caring for people and things.**

To any of us who are familiar with the terrible plight of much of Eastern Europe after decades of communism, one fact is self-evident: Without the responsible stewardship of private property and personal initiative, the ability for self-rule and productivity is lost. This is the practical message of socialism. It destroys man's rulership capacities. And since God has called us to be kings[1] (rulers) and priests (intercessors), anything that destroys or blunts either possibility is not from God.

God makes us grow up by giving us responsibility, and responsibility begins with exercising authority over some one, some talent, or some task. Without responsibility, I would put very little truth into practice. The measure of my maturity is how I care for what God has entrusted to me.

As we have already seen, God has placed us in His earthly workshop to both make us grow up and to extend His Kingdom here in the process. The obstacles that are within us and outside of us form the "barbells" we must pump in life in order to grow spiritual muscles. All of us have heard the saying, "no pain, no gain." It's true. Pumping responsibility and personal growth is the training routine of both the Lord Jesus,[2] and all the franchise's junior partners who follow Him. Personal gifts, private property, and human relationships form the heart of what God expects us to use in exercising our spiritual muscles.

---

[1] 1 Peter 2:9
[2] Heb. 5:8

In this chapter we will deal with four major muscle-making concepts: (1) the nature of property and increase, (2) joint labor—the secret of true fellowship, (3) the nature of power and our ability to handle it, and (4) the cardinal rule of biblical management—good leaders produce proprietors.

### Responsibility and Producing Increase Makes Us Grow Up

In Luke 19:12-27, Jesus taught another one of His many parables dealing with business and stewardship, but this one is especially pointed: If we neglect to give Him back increase on those things He has entrusted to us, we are in big trouble. Let's read some of the parable together:

> He said therefore, "A certain nobleman went to a distant country to receive a kingdom for himself and then return. And he called ten of his slaves and gave them ten minas, and said to them, 'Do business with this until I come back.'

> "But his citizens hated him and sent a delegation after him saying, 'We do not want this man to reign over us.'

> "And it came about that when he returned after receiving the kingdom, he ordered that these slaves, to whom he had given the money, be called to him in order that he might know what business they had done.

> "And the first appeared, saying 'Master, your mina has made ten minas more.'

> "And he said to him, 'Well done, good slave, because you have been faithful in a very little thing, be in authority over ten cities.'

> "And the second came saying, 'Your mina, master, has made five minas.'

> "And he said to him also, 'And you are to be over five cities.'

"And another came, saying, 'Master, behold your mina, which I kept put away in a handkerchief; for I was afraid of you, because you are an exacting man; you take up what you did not lay down, and reap what you did not sow.'

"He said to him, 'By your own words I will judge you, you worthless slave. Did you know that I am an exacting man, taking up what I did not lay down, and reaping what I did not sow? Then why did you not put the money in the bank, and having come, I would have collected it with interest?' And he said to the bystanders, 'Take the mina away from him and give it to the one who has the ten minas.'

"And they said to him, 'Master, he has ten minas already.'

"He replied, 'I tell you, that to everyone who has shall *more* be given, but from the one who does not have, even what he does have shall be taken away.'"

Remember, He owns all things. Verses 22 and 23, where he addresses the "worthless slave," are especially tough verses; God demands increase on what He loans to us!

### The Five Things for Which All People Must Give an Account

What are some of the things God has given to all of us, regardless of how our personal balance sheet reads? He has given all of us at least five assets for which we will have to answer to Christ regarding their stewardship:

1. Our physical bodies
2. Our conscience
3. Our relationships with others
4. Our talents
5. Our possessions

All of these items are on loan from God, and we are to deal with them under the stewardship of God's Word and bring them back to Him with increase.

Again, if you have nothing under your care, you will never grow up. Growth is directly related to responsibility. The first judgment we will all face is for what we do in our bodies.[3] Our bodies are our first assigned stewardship, and we progress from there. Every human has one. The question will be, did we steward our body morally and according to God's Word? The second thing we must give an account for is our conscience. The Puritans and other historically reformed groups considered the conscience to be God's most important gift. To build one's conscience up in God's Word and keep it pure was the highest of stewardship issues.

Thirdly, our God-ordained relationships and their care, development, and stewardship is so very important that Jesus made it a major issue as He reported back to the Father during His earthly stewardship report in John 17, just prior to His death. Look at these verses:

> **John 17:6**
> I manifested Thy name to the men whom Thou gavest Me out of the world; Thine they were, and Thou gavest them to Me, and they have kept Thy word.

> **John 17:8**
> For the words which Thou gavest Me I have given to them; and they received them, and truly understood that I came forth from Thee, and they believed that Thou didst send me.

> **John 17:9**
> I ask on their behalf; I do not ask on behalf of the world, but of those whom Thou hast given Me; for they are Thine.

---

[3] 2 Cor. 5:10

**John 17:11**
And I am no more in the world; and yet they themselves are in the world, and I come to Thee. Holy Father, keep them in Thy name, the name which Thou hast given Me, that they may be one, even as We are.

**John 17:12**
While I was with them, I was keeping them in Thy name which Thou hast given Me; and I guarded them, and not one of them perished but the son of perdition, that the Scripture might be fulfilled.

**John 17:15-20**
I do not ask Thee to take them out of the world, but to keep them from the evil one. They are not of the world, even as I am not of the world. Sanctify them in the truth; Thy word is truth. As Thou didst send Me into the world, I also have sent them into the world. And for their sakes I sanctify Myself, that they themselves also may be sanctified in truth. I do not ask in behalf of these alone, but for those also who believe in Me through their word.

Indeed, virtually the whole of the "prayer report" is about Christ's relationships and His stewardship of them. All successful lives and organizations ultimately end up focusing on relational stewardship. Father's franchise is built relationally, and so are well-run business enterprises.

Fourthly, we are similarly to steward and bring increase to our God-given talents. Whatever we have we are to build upon and develop. What skills have you been given? How about your family members? How about your business colleagues? What are you doing to serve these people by drawing out and developing their skills and wisdom? A Christian business isn't simply an honest business or one that properly pays its taxes: even many non-Christians do that. No, a Christian business is one that is primarily committed to developing human beings because that is the business our Father is in—developing human beings. Proverbs 20:5 clearly makes this statement about the commitment to personal development found in a godly enterprise: "A plan in the heart of a man is like deep water, but a man of understanding draws it out." Good leaders, especially in business, help their colleagues discover the plans and visions God has put into their hearts.

Fifthly, maturation in stewardship of possessions is a major part of all our training in our spiritual lives. Good leaders help their people become better stewards. Jesus revealed three principles about growing in maturity as stewards when He said these words:

> He that is faithful in that which is least is faithful also in much: and he that is unjust in the least is unjust also in much. If therefore ye have not been faithful in the unrighteous mammon, who will commit to your trust the true riches? And if ye have not been faithful in that which is another man's, who shall give you that which is your own?
>
> *Luke 16:10-12 (KJV)*

You grow: (1) from small to large, (2) from natural to spiritual, and (3) from managing someone else's things to managing your own.

Since the ownership of property is so vital to spiritual maturity, it's critical that we do the following for our children: get them picking up their rooms by the time they're three or so, give them allowances, get them buying their own clothes, and get them into a personal stewardship program as early as we can. That is far more important than teaching them to memorize ideas or concepts they don't know how to use. Our whole lives are a long study in how responsible we are, and what we do with what we have. Obviously, the sooner we can get this into our children, the better off they are. Indeed, aren't morals nothing more than the good stewardship of entrusted gifts?

All of these concepts have profound implications in terms of building families, businesses, and nations. Suffice it to say that these God-ordained laws of stewardship and increase are to have profound effects on a nation's welfare and public care policies. These laws of stewardship should also shape business decisions relative to both personal promotions and capital outlay for department or project spending.

## The Secret of Deepening Fellowship Is Building Things Together

God, as a wise Employer/Father, brings His servants into mature fellowship with Himself by making them His work partners. The old adage, "It takes one to know one," is not only true, but it's also biblical.[4] In the same way that it takes an architect to read an architect's plans, it takes someone fully engaged in Father's business to really begin to know Him. Unity comes from sharing goals, responsibility, and time together.

God's original intent for man has never changed. He wants us to build together in the extension of His will and His ways throughout the created order He has entrusted man to steward.[5] Indeed, it is truly awe-inspiring that He has tuned the created order to respond to man's care for it. The created order will not be free from sin's bondage until man begins to steward it properly. Listen to Paul saying exactly this in Romans 8, verses 19 through 21:

> For the anxious longing of the creation
> waits eagerly for the revealing of the sons
> of God. For the creation was subjected to
> futility, not of its own will, but because of
> Him who subjected it, in hope that the
> creation itself also will be set free from its
> slavery to corruption into the freedom of the
> glory of the children of God.

God's fellowship with man began in the garden as He discussed Adam's work in the cool of the day; it may well extend to distant galaxies in the future for all we know. One thing is for sure: We'll be

---

[4] Psa. 18:26
[5] Gen. 1:26-28

together working with Him because common work and building things together is the heart of sharing true life and biblical covenant.

When Jesus first invited us into fellowship with Him, it was through working together, not sitting and chatting. Listen carefully to what He says: "Come to Me, all who are weary and heavy laden, and I will give you rest. Take my yoke upon you and learn from Me; for I am gentle and humble in heart; and you shall find rest for your souls. For My yoke is easy and My load is light" (Matt. 11:28-30).

Please take note of the admonition to stick your head in "His yoke," for it's there you particularly "learn of Him." It is in the yoke of God's business that we learn to see His goals, learn His ways of operation, discern reality, sweat out our sins and impurities, recruit others, and fellowship with Him in our victories and defeats. The rocking chair just inside the north gate of Heaven may make for tears and emotional singing, but it's the work assignment in God's Kingdom that makes good disciples! God is into work, and in chapter four we'll see more of why this is so.

The scripture says, "The heavens are the heavens of the Lord, but the Earth He has given to the sons of men."[6] It is here on Earth that man has been given the opportunity both now and in the future to work out his divine partnership with God, both in this age and in the age to come.[7] When we buy into ALMIGHTY & SONS, we are buying into God's business and God's destiny. This is the inheritance in us that Paul begged us to see and consider in Ephesians 1:18-22. God's inheritance in us is a shared life and a shared rulership over His projects. What a God, what a Creator, and what an Entrepreneur we have! Yes, deep biblical fellowship comes from shared dreams, plans, methods, and investments. And God the Businessman and Entrepreneur knows it well.

---

[6] Psa. 115:16
[7] Rev. 21:10

## God's Co-Workers Are Learning to Share Power Gradually So That It Doesn't Destroy Them

Man's problem is that God put a high-powered Corvette engine in a Model A frame: God's power plant far exceeds our puny capacities to contain and utilize it. Our character, until forged and purified through trials and problems, is too weak and self-serving to handle much power without being corrupted. God must therefore train us to incrementally handle His power, lest we be destroyed by the very thing we most need to work with Him. Little by little we learn to handle in Christ what Satan and those who follow him have only been corrupted by, that is, more power than their character could handle.

## Power Is Guarded by Problems

Power sharing comes through problem solving. Our problems qualify us for more and more spiritual responsibility, and with responsibility comes God's power. "Power" can be defined as sharing knowledge, ability, and authority with God over some portion of His creation. Problems have a wonderful way of cleansing us from selfish ambition, presumption, and ignorance. Problems often "beat the hell out of us," and properly so.

It would require a book in itself to do this subject justice. Suffice to say, in this introductory study of biblical management principles, God, as the Master Leader, promotes "problem solvers" rather than people who merely have potential. All the heroes of the Bible are problem solvers. Analyzing those heroes, their problems, and how they solved them, is an unbelievably useful way to study God's Word. Try it sometime as the point of departure for a leadership class or business team discussion group. Wise leaders promote and produce problem solvers, because they are skilled problem solvers themselves. The so-called "Peter Principle," promoting people up to their level of incompetency, is a perfect illustration of my point. Our leadership stops at the point where we can no longer solve the problems.

The parable of the Prodigal Son (Luke 15:11-32) illustrates the tragedy of giving someone power before he has the character to handle it. Reread this parable and run it through this gridwork of understanding; it will come to life! If you're like most businessmen, you've had times when you've promoted somebody and then wished you'd never done it. You gave power or responsibility based on *potential,* rather than faithfulness. God doesn't do that. In God's family business, power comes only on the basis of faithfulness. That's why problems are the doorway to power and authority. They stimulate courage, creativity, dependence on God, knowledge, patience, tenacity, and teamwork in us. They build and reveal character. How an employee handles a problem will tell you more about his character than scores of instant successes. Someone who handles problems faithfully will be good for your business in the long-run. God releases resources to people qualified to handle them. Those whose power or "anointing" exceed their character often end up disgraced or in jail. Problem solving forces upon us the issue of self-government along with personal and relational discipline. It reveals the ability to solve relational as well as conceptual blockages.

Put another way, God only trusts those He has processed through problems. And problems are in fact a form of "property," that is, something we own. Irresponsibility means not properly stewarding what truly belongs to you, including your problems. We need to remember that God is far more interested in getting His heavenly perspective into us than in getting us into Heaven.

## Good Leaders Produce Proprietors

Poor leadership or poor government produces welfarism, dependency, confusion, apathy, carelessness, and debt. Good government or able leadership produces the exact opposite in every case. Godly leadership has one primary serving goal: to draw others into their full potential in God.[8]

Everything God has created or birthed has an inherent design or pattern. "Success" is found in drawing that design out, and then revealing and developing it. God's design for individuals, families,

---

[8] Luke 22:24-26

churches, businesses, and even nations must determine how wise leaders govern. Good leaders help those they lead to discover their God-given talents and destiny (property from God) and to fulfill them.[9] Nothing that is out of order or missing God's design and purposes can prosper in the long-run. Good leaders produce the proprietorial spirit in others that encourages in them a sense of personal stake, property, and ownership in their life and activities. And this truth comes from God, not the Harvard M.B.A. program or anyone else. Leading people into ownership is the key to their growth and success.

## God Wants All His Kids to Own a Piece of the Action

What distinguishes being a partner from being merely an employee is authority. In an employer/employee relationship, the employer has all the authority, or power. In a partnership, the members share power. God wants us to be *partners* in ALMIGHTY & SONS, not mere employees.

Nonetheless, many Christians lack the power God wants them to have, whether in their families, in their businesses, or in any other part of their lives. They lack it largely because they hope to gain it by the wrong means. They pray, "Oh, God, give me power!" But they get problems, and so they give up. They don't understand that God is answering their prayer. The Holy Spirit uses problems to teach us how to properly apply God's Word and how to appropriate true faith. This principle is similarly evident in the same way that a senior partner in a business grooms junior partners by giving them increasingly difficult responsibilities. Many businessmen want profitable businesses without problems. That is not a Christian approach to business. God sends problems to strengthen His junior partners so He can give them more power.

If you want Father's guaranteed blessing on what you're doing, you will make it a top priority to discover the gifts of those who work with you, saved or unsaved, and draw them into what God created

---

[9] Phil. 3:12; Acts 17:26

them to be—not mere employees, but members of the divine partnership of ALMIGHTY & SONS. You are about Father's business. As you begin to reach into people's lives and discern their gifts, by the power of the Spirit, and help them to discover and fulfill their calling, the unsaved will get saved, and the saved will grow in maturity. That is what economic evangelism and discipleship is all about. It is building according to Father's pattern, and it is what businessmen and parents are called to do.

God hasn't called us primarily to make money. He has called us to work with Him in building character skills and relationships with people. These things will pass on into the next age. Paul tells us in 1 Cor. 3:9-15 that our work is going to be tested by fire. The fire will evaluate whether what we've built is wood, hay and stubble, or gold, silver, and precious stones. Hear us, brothers and sisters! Hear us, business people! Hear us, lawyers and C.P.A.'s! Father is not after your accumulating houses and boats and stock portfolios. These are all fine; there's nothing wrong with them. But they will not get into the casket with you and pass through the fire. What will pass through the fire are your character skills and your capacity for obedience in faith.

People say, "Joe Smith died last week. He had a tremendous Christian testimony. He left $5 billion in trust." Great! But what did he take with him? Did he take eternal work skills that Father can use in the next phase of his life, or was he simply a "Christian businessman" who made a lot of money?

Now, I pray that you'll make a lot of money and spend it wisely, but that isn't my goal in this book. My goal is to get Christian business and professional people to see that we must build eternal things in our character and skills and impart them into our business associates, partners, and employees alike, because only those things will pass through the fire. I'll talk about this principle in detail in chapter four when I discuss "work."

Your business may or may not survive your death. What will go on after you die is the combination of character skills (the stewardship) that you've first developed in yourself and then stimulated in others.

That will pass on in the extension of ALMIGHTY & SONS. While God values profitable increase, He values character development far more. Possessions do not pass with us through death. Only character skills go with us into eternity: godly motives, godly ethics, service orientation, leadership skill, and stewardship skills. These pass through the fire.

## Character Generates Profit

No doubt, when you grapple with all the problems in your business, you'll be tempted just to look to the bottom line. But God wants your continual prayer to be, "Father, teach me to handle these problems by the Book. Give me faithfulness and understanding, because when this business is gone, and with it all that I've given to charity, what will last is the character and skills I have developed and imparted to those with whom I work."

Imagine the impact five or ten thousand Christian business people with that ethic could have on your nation. They would radically transform whatever they touched.

Along the way, they'd generate a lot of profit, because people never work harder than when they work for themselves, and your goal is to get as many people in your business working for _themselves_ as you can. That's where profit is generated. We are trying to mobilize people in their businesses and professions to see that as their primary call.

The master principle of this chapter centers around the text that God fellowships with man by giving us stewardship over His possessions, making them "our" property. May God anoint you to clearly hear this truth, to study it, to read over and over the scriptures I've cited, and then to go into your Kiwanis Club, your Lions Club, or your Chamber of Commerce and start recruiting for your private little spiritual revolution in your community, to begin imparting these principles into the community. The unsaved have no future apart from building the way God builds. Our Christian responsibility is to instruct them in how to do this by modeling these truths in our personal lives, our professional lives, and in the witness of our churches.

Good leaders produce co-workers, and co-workers come to maturity because they have a sense of personally owning and improving what has been entrusted to them.

*"For we are God's fellow workers..."* 1 Cor. 3:9

# CHAPTER THREE

# Generational Wealth and the Family Unit

*"For a child will be born to us, a son will be given to us; and the government will rest on His shoulders; and His name will be called Wonderful Counselor, Mighty God, Eternal Father, Prince of Peace."*                    Isaiah 9:6

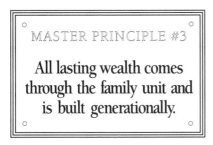

MASTER PRINCIPLE #3

**All lasting wealth comes through the family unit and is built generationally.**

ALMIGHTY & SONS (& DAUGHTERS) is a family operation. Why? Because God is a family man. He works through the family and is connected to the structure of the family. We are born again into a relationship with Him as our Father, and with fellow Christians as brothers and sisters who are being apprenticed into co-running the family business. That apprenticeship is about responsibility, stewardship, and "buying in" to God's work and people. When properly growing, we are growing in love, which means growing in commitment to our Father, His Creation, and what He is doing. I love God for what Christ "saved me from," but I love Him even more for what He "saved me into." He saved me into His family (relationships) and business (opportunity to use all my God-ordained gifts and motivation to their fullest). To be in love with my Father without a focused goal, would result in a peculiar kind of emptiness.

## Use It or Lose It

Jesus announced a major spiritual law, which we will deal with in more detail in chapter nine, on how increase and prosperity work in His Kingdom: "For whoever has, to him shall more be given, and he shall have an abundance; but whoever does not have, even what he has shall be taken away from him" (Matt. 13:12). This principle establishes this truth: Those who care for what they have been given get more, and those who misuse what they have, lose it. That is roughly what we mean when we say, "Use it or lose it." A lot of slang is based on Bible truths. What are we to use? We use our "wealth," which all of us have, and our "riches," which all of us have in varying measures. So what is the difference between "wealth" and "riches," and why do I assert that all lasting wealth comes through the family unit and is built generationally?

## A Quick Look at Wealth and Riches

While "wealth" and "riches" will be discussed in greater detail in the next chapter, we have to introduce the issue now since their linkage to the family unit and generational strategic planning is inseparable. In order to make an important distinction, I am using others' definition of "riches" as *perishable assets* which Christ warned us not to improperly focus upon as the primary goal of our labors.[1] Riches can be initially gained with or without ethics and morals. "Wealth," on the other hand, is primarily achieved through the skills, spiritual knowledge, and character developed in obeying God's ways of approaching resource management. Riches are something we have; wealth is something we are. Our job is to put our hearts into what is a treasure to God, which is the wealth He has for us in Christ. Then we properly let the riches that God chooses to give us take their appointed course in our lives according to our calling. Wealth will pass through death, but riches will not.[2]

There are five major areas of biblically definable wealth: (1) relational peace with God, (2) relationships God has given you, (3) revelational wealth, (4) time, and (5) material contentment. All these attributes of wealth are to be carefully studied and taught from parents to children and generation to generation. It is the work of the family business to build wealth across the generations. All good parents seek to do so. ALMIGHTY & SONS is an eternally expanding enterprise because God is multiplying His vision and "work project" across the generations of man, and through time.[3]

---

[1] Matt. 6:20
[2] 1 Cor. 3:9-15; Matt. 6:19-20
[3] Isa. 9:7

## The Basic Wealth-Generating Unit in Scripture Is the Family

*"And I will bless those who bless you, and the one who curses you I will curse. And in you all the families of the earth shall be blessed."* Gen. 12:3

*"It is you who are the sons of the prophets, and of the covenant which God made with your fathers, saying to Abraham, 'And in your seed all the families of the earth shall be blessed.'"* Acts 3:25

God's blessing pipeline is the family unit; that is why the warfare around our families is often so severe. If you weaken or destroy the family, you cut the pipeline of wealth, and usually the next generation starts in the hole, not "even." The poverty of America's inner cities is a living example of this tragedy. Our spiritual family line, humanly speaking, begins with father Abraham.[4] The Jews rightly understood the centrality of being in Abraham's line in relation to salvation.[5] God told Abraham that stewarding his family and its wealth, by governing righteously, was central to his being able to walk through life in God's covenant promises:

> ...since Abraham will surely become a
> great and mighty nation, and in him all the
> nations of the earth will be blessed. For I
> have chosen him, in order that he may
> command his children and his household
> after him to keep the way of the Lord by
> doing righteousness and justice; in order
> that the Lord may bring upon Abraham
> what He has spoken about him.   *Gen. 18:18-19*

Please note the little phrase, "in order that." In other words, if Abraham blew it at home, there went the pipeline of wealth to the nations. Talk about family pressure!

Family government at home produces wealth, and that wealth of skills, talent, and stewardship flows from the front doors of the homes like small trickles of little streams and eventually becomes collective rivers for the nations to bathe in. Put another way, if wealth is not

---

[4] Rom. 4:16
[5] Matt. 3:9

coming from the family units, then neither Washington, D.C., Tokyo, or Bonn can produce it.

Our children are a stewardship, a heritage, and an inheritance from the Lord.[6] God requires us to pass on our wealth to them and to raise them in the faith as we teach them the truths and moral wealth-creating principles of scripture.[7]

If you want to know why we're excited about the concepts of this book, it's because we love our children and the idea of restoring godly stewardship, not only in our own families but across each nation and around the world. It is an essential part of the inheritance we hope to leave them. That's the deepest motivation we have to spread these concepts. We're looking ahead to the children's good.

### One Way to Tell If You Love Your Children: What Is Their Inheritance?

In His high priestly prayer in John 17, Jesus exemplified the attitude of relational stewardship which God wants to instill in each of His children. Christ reported back to God on how He had managed the people and affairs the Father had sent Him to oversee. As we've seen already, He acknowledged that everything He had came from and ultimately belonged to the Father (verses 7-10). He confirmed that He had carefully preserved and built up that inheritance (verses 12-14). Then He prayed that, upon His departure from them, the Father would continue to preserve them, to sanctify and build them up, and to multiply them (verses 15-21).

These three elements—receiving an inheritance, preserving and building that inheritance, and passing that inheritance on to future generations—form the backbone of a biblical understanding of faithful stewardship of wealth and responsibilities, whether physical or spiritual. It begins with the humble acknowledgment that whatever we start with, we owe to others and ultimately to God.[8] It rises to the challenge of multiplying what we receive, not for our own

---

[6] Psa. 127
[7] Deut. 6:6-9
[8] 1 Cor. 4:7

consumption, but for the glory of God and the service of others.[9] It climaxes in our passing on to coming generations the fruit of our labors, in accordance with Proverbs 13:22: "A good man leaves an inheritance to his children's children..."

John Maynard Keynes, our economic system's father, was no family man. He was a homosexual, and he didn't think about children. Keynes' immorality totally shaped his fiscal and monetary theories. Once, when he was asked what would be the long-run effect of his tax-and-spend and inflationary policies, he replied lightheartedly, "In the long-run, we're all dead."

Everybody tittered and said, "Heavy existential thinker here!!"

Now, fifty years later, people are beginning to say, "Hey, the long-run is here, and now what are we going to do? Why should we be the ones who are dead because Keynes and his single generational thinking promoted the eating up of tomorrow's assets today?"

If you don't love your children, your economics will tend to be debt based and consumption based. Then, like any good Keynesian economist, you will pile up debt and shove it down the road. If you love your children, you won't do that, because the Bible says parents ought to leave equity, not debt, for their children to inherit.[10] The person or society that piles up debt is acting with hate toward their children.

Can you see a causal connection between abortion and debt financing? They spring from the same spirit. When the United States, if God helps us, terminates abortion on demand, then corporate debt/equity structures will begin to change as well, because they're causally linked. The hatred of children, coupled with a willingness to kill them for our convenience or to pile up future debt upon them for the sake of our immediate consumption, causes both abortion and debt-leveraged financing.

---

[9] Psa. 90:16-17
[10] 2 Cor. 12:14

You cannot separate ethical issues from economic issues, "For where your treasure is, there your heart will be also."[11] Our economic choices reflect our hearts' values. If we act with hate toward our children, it'll show up in our finances.

## We Must Learn to Build Multi-Generationally

Lasting wealth is multi-generational, and it's oriented toward the long-run, not the short-run. Remember, God is the God of Abraham, Isaac, and Jacob. That's the three generation principle. As a general rule, whatever God builds endures at least three generations. And as a rule, it takes at least three generations for a major character trait to be implanted, or replaced, in a family.

My great-grandfather once cut a winter's worth of wood, stacked it up next to the barn and deserted the family for twenty-five years. When he came back, he gave a British gold sovereign to my grandmother, who passed it on to my dad, who finally gave it to me. I had the coin made into a ring because it means so much to me. It reminds me that the curse I saw operating through my great-grandfather also had its effect on my grandfather and my father. The curse of desertion that brought such great harm to their families ends in *my* generation. I am determined to leave a lasting inheritance to my children's children, and the ring on my finger is my reminder. My prayer now is that God will permit me to build, through my children and grandchildren, three generations of family stewardship that will contribute mightily to the growth of the Kingdom of the God of Abraham, Isaac, and Jacob.

The curse of poverty is single generational wealth. It is selfishness versus heritage. It is consumption versus savings. Inheritance tax and anti-family practices produce poverty. Some years ago I was told that Japanese corporate executives had bought large blocks of land in the Amazon rain forest. Why? Not primarily for profit, but to save the environment for their children! Whatever the actual long-range realities of this situation turn out to be, the intent of these executives was

---

[11]Matt. 6:21

right, and when we learned of this it sent us into mourning. Why are the Japanese acting as stewards of God's creation instead of Christian businessmen and women? How do you witness to a heathen who loves his children like that? The Japanese look at us as a "Christian nation" and say, "Thanks, but no thanks. We're not interested in that; we've got more going than you do."

We must change the perspective of our families, businesses, communities, and nations to long-range thinking. Saving and investment, not consumption and debt, must drive our economy.

Godly families pass on the skills of stewardship and character as the primary guarantee of success: They don't emphasize things or money. Any man who wants his successful business to remain successful for generations to come, and to stay in the hands of the family, must train up his children to take over that business. They must understand the spirit that brings success: a long-run vision, care for people and relationship building, and an overall understanding that they are stewards accountable to God for how they handle everything He gives them.

We have no idea how much we're going to leave to our children. We hope that, if Christ tarries, God will allow us to leave them something. But do you want to know what we really care about? We don't care much about leaving them things. We care about leaving them character skills, because someone with character skills can acquire all the things he needs. But someone who has "things" without character skills can't even hold onto those things, much less acquire more. More importantly, all the things we pass on, and all the things our children acquire because of their character skills, will be burned up in the fire. Only the character skills will pass through to eternity.

Many think that you have to inherit riches to be wealthy. Wrong! According to George Gilder, "The vast majority of American's fortunes are dissipated within two generations." Why? "When the money is actually passed on, [much of it] ends up among large numbers of prodigal sons and daughters...The receipt of a legacy, it turns out, often erodes the qualities of entrepreneurship that are needed to perpetuate it."[12]

The mistake many rich people make is neglecting to teach their children to be wealthy. So, when the children inherit the money, they waste it, spending it foolishly or investing in fools' projects.

The pattern of Jesus' high priestly prayer is the key to avoiding that waste: first cultivate wise stewardship in ourselves, and then (through example, precept, and practice) cultivate it in our children. No one can achieve godly, mature character without being responsible for the wise and faithful stewardship of private property.

We believe God wants to raise up Christian dynasties, families who teach their children from one generation to the next and build a snowball of wealth to use for God's Kingdom. But that will only happen as God's people learn, by the disciplined practice of managing private property, to be good stewards.

Riches gained quickly are soon lost.[13] Why? Because if you gain too many riches too quickly, you won't have the skills to manage them. That's why those who get rich quickly rarely stay rich for long. Accumulating riches is not based on how fast you get it. It's based on the ability to manage what you get responsibly. That's why gambling and get-rich-quick schemes never do anybody any good in the long-run. It's why all the quick money-raising ideas church leaders come up with to finance their ministries, and the lotteries that more and more states are using to shore up their finances, will never work in the long-run. ALMIGHTY & SONS doesn't work that way.

Remember when the Israelites took the Promised Land? Moses said, "And the Lord your God will clear away these nations before you little by little; you will not be able to put an end to them quickly, lest the wild beasts grow too numerous for you."[14] The principle is simple: Don't take more than you can manage.

---

[12] George Gilder, *Wealth and Poverty* (New York: Bantam Books, 1981) pp. 76,74
[13] Prov. 20:21
[14] Deut. 7:22

Investing in relationships is the key to wealth since it promotes covenantal responses (self-government) rather than short-run consumption. Christ's last act before His death was to arrange for the care of His family.[15] What a wonderful example for all of us to follow!

## Economic Prosperity Is Based on the Family Unit

A nation's economic prosperity is based upon its view of and care for the family unit. Good family law is good economic policy for a nation for a legion of reasons. We can only touch on a few of them in an introductory study like this. Suffice it to say, since the wealth generating skills within the family unit determine a nation's collective wealth and riches, laws or policies that are anti-family/anti-biblical are also economically suicidal. Cripple the family, and you destroy the national economy.

Divorce, illegitimacy policies, abortion, pornography, and materialism show up directly in a nation's savings rate, debt-equity structures, civic and corporate debt, and nonreplenishable resource consumption. The best barometer of the United States' economic health is not the Dow Jones industrial average or the unemployment rate. It is the rate of improvement or regression of the state of the family, and that is a spiritual and moral affair. Economics *is* about family. Its root word "oikos" literally means "household management."

## As the Family Goes, So Goes the Nation

If the culture within a nation is single generational in its view of life, that attitude will clearly show up economically in a, "let's spend it now" attitude, rather than planning to lay up for our Isaacs and Jacobs of the second and third generations. The same is true for business. Selfishness produces low savings rates, both personal and corporate. Dividends will also tend to be high, and profits earmarked for research and development and future market share will be inadequate. Abortion

---

[15] John 19:26-27

rates will be high. It will be legal, due to a "convenience" orientation which prevents us from seeing our children as "arrows" we shoot across time into the future. All of these anti-family attitudes have economically shown up in the United States.

United States savings rates in relation to gross domestic product are the lowest in the industrialized world, at this point about one-third of Japan's, and the over emphasis on corporate dividends has made future market-share policies a joke. Add to this tax policies that refuse to adequately encourage investment capital through appropriate investment tax credits, and you have a national policy reflecting selfish parents (or lawmakers) which can only severely penalize future generations. When fathers and mothers no longer think of long-term wealth accumulation and think only of short-term consumption, the curse begins to flow economically, and it is already flowing in this nation. When men are obsessed with pornography, which sets up absurd physical comparisons between eighteen-year-old beauties and moms with stretch marks on their stomachs, adultery and a loss of generational sacrifice is inevitable.

Broken families and the resulting unstable work force are inevitable in a society that believes it has a right to no-fault divorce. Ultimately, when people are motivated by selfishness, they destroy cooperation and create poverty. They lose their lives spending them only on themselves.[16] Absenteeism, ascending health care costs, and a general lack of product quality is the result. More than anything else, economics is about people's motivations and generational choices. Sadly, long-lasting fruit, in a day of maximized, short-run dividends, is almost unthinkable in contemporary America. Americans, having lost their Christian base, no longer think about wealth in the long-run. Everything is short-run. We always attempt to maximize short-run returns, even when the long-run consequences are disastrous. But Jesus says, "By this is My Father glorified, that you bear much fruit"— fruit that remains.[17]

---

[16] Matt. 10:39
[17] John 15:8, 16

### The Christian Message of Free Enterprise Is Essential

Our failures are in both the public and the private sectors. In the public sector, burgeoning government debt bespeaks the short-run mentality, ignoring the mounting interest costs that rob the government of the funds it needs to perform vital services. The short-run mentality also drives government giveaway programs, whether to the poor (welfare, food stamps, subsidized housing, etc.) or to the rich and middle class (big business bailouts, "free" education, pork barrel spending, commodity price subsidies, trade protectionism, etc.). All such measures are shortsighted, designed to relieve short-term distress with a price tag of long-term slavery.

That's why we have to multiply this message. The Lions Club doesn't have the moral fuel to promote private property and family based economic policies. It doesn't have the understanding. The Kiwanis Club doesn't. The Chamber of Commerce doesn't. They all say private property and free enterprise are good. Why? They don't know. Maybe because they make people rich. But if the last twenty or thirty years have taught us anything, they've taught us that being rich doesn't necessarily mean being either happy or virtuous.

So why are private property and free enterprise good? Because giving people things to steward helps them become mature. It sets them free from the prisons of poverty and tyranny and single generation thinking. It forces people to steward things and grow up, and to think of the consequences of their choices on their posterity. It's that simple.

Nehemiah, in a time of great crisis, reached down into the souls of the men to find their ultimate motivation and resolve. He knew where to find it. Do we?

> When I saw their fear, I rose and spoke to
> the nobles, the officials, and the rest of the
> people: "Do not be afraid of them; remember
> the Lord who is great and awesome, and fight
> for your brothers, your sons, your daughters,
> your wives, and your houses." *Neh. 4:14*

I cannot leave this section without making a related comment relative to family economics and private property. God has given land to only two institutions: nations (Acts 17:26) and families (Lev. chapter 25; Lev. 27:24). When Israel entered the Promised Land, God didn't give the civil government one inch of land. He distributed all of it to families. He ensured that it would stay with families by enacting the Jubilee law which limited the duration of land sales to fifty years, after which land had to revert to the original family owners.

In contrast, the federal government is the largest single landowner in the United States, but no verse of scripture authorizes civil government to own land. Eminent domain is not a right or a pillar of society, but an exception to the rule. The rule is private property owners may use their land and all their property as they please, as long as they don't harm other people.[18]

Unfortunately, the modern state seems determined to undermine the very lessons of stewardship necessary to produce mature people. Whether by unjustly taxing away hard-earned wealth and inheritance, or by giving people wealth to consume without accountability, it is eroding both the right and the responsibility of private property, and thereby undermining the important connection between private property and stewardship.

If we want our children and grandchildren to learn good stewardship, we must meet and overcome that challenge.

### Generational Thinking Requires Us to Think Strategically

God is a strategic thinker. His revelation of this fact came to me in the summer of 1987 and changed my life and ministry. Let me share with you how that change began.

Sitting in the back yard at lunch I was tired and discouraged. I had spoken to possibly thirty thousand people already that year, but I realized that speaking to people and helping to change people are not

---

[18] Matt. 20:15; Acts 5:4

always the same thing. "God," I said, "You've got to show me another way; I refuse to become simply a Christian entertainer."

The Lord answered, "Dennis, I want you to begin to relate to Me as an investment banker."

"What?" I asked.

"I want you to put as much time and planning into the projects you want Me to bless as you would if you took them to a worldly banker. If you took most of your projects to a worldly banker, he'd laugh you out of the office if you didn't come with perk charts, if you couldn't demonstrate that you had the management skill and ability to return his investment. Don't bring Me plans on which you haven't even done the same research you would do if you were going to a worldly banker for backing."

Who but a businessman could relate to that? Say that to pastors, and they'll think you've lost your marbles! How many Christian leaders relate to God as an investment banker? Yet that simple word changed my life. It taught me that God wants us to demonstrate good stewardship by wise, strategic planning. Why? Because strategic planning produces wealth and lasting increase, and those are things God wants to share with us.

God is a long-range planner who thinks from the end to the beginning. His family business was perfectly planned before He created a single molecule of this Earth.[19] The closer we get to God, the more we think the way He does, generationally and strategically.[20]

### Strategic Thinking: The Art of the True Leader

Under God's grace, prosperity and success are fruits of strategic planning and obedience, not the goal. Strategic planning requires that we be oriented to the future generation on these three issues:

---

[19] Psa. 139:16; Isa. 46:10; Eph. 1:4; 2 Tim. 1:9; Rev. 13, 17:8
[20] Out of this change in my life, I did a seminar tape series called "Strategic Thinking." We have sold more of these tapes than any others to leaders.

1. What is God's overall work for my generation so my life work can fit into it?

2. What is my calling, and how does it relate to the destiny of my children?

3. What wealth and riches (resource base) has God entrusted to me to multiply and pass on into godly hands?

As you can tell, these are not simple questions, and they require an investment of *time and prayer* to be properly handled. True strategic thinkers become problem solvers relative to the future.

Many investors think foreseeing the future is a deep mystery. In reality, it rests on seeing the present through Christ-oriented eyes. Specifically, it rests on identifying people and businesses with a heart of servanthood. Why? Because God promises to exalt humble, service-oriented people.[21]

One of the first principles of a successful business is Henry Kaiser's old dictum, "Find a need and fill it." Whoever meets people's needs will prosper. God wants to raise up Christian men and women with servants' hearts and the foresight to know where to invest what God has given them. Where does wealth naturally gravitate? Toward servants. We'll make this point again. Strategic thinkers see where people's true needs are going and execute plans to meet them there with what they need.

God is also looking for Christian business and professional people who can promote self-government, proprietorship, and teamwork: people like the late Sam Walton of Wal-Mart Stores.

Part of being self-governing in business is being strongly capitalized, not leveraged. Why? Because "the rich rule over the poor, and the borrower is servant to the lender."[22] When hard times come, companies that have financed their growth internally are much healthier than companies that are leveraged up to their eyeballs. A lot of people

---

[21] Phil. 2:5-11; 1 Peter 5:6
[22] Prov. 22:7 (KJV)

got rich in the Great Depression because they had never borrowed. Many get rich through any downturn if they follow biblical principles and stick with them.

## Five Categories of Wealth Stewardship We Should Teach Our Children

When you look to see what God has put into your hand, and what He intends you to steward for His Kingdom, keep in mind five categories of wealth that He might put there.

1) **Real wealth begins with a biblical perspective on life.**
   No matter how much money you have, if you don't see reality according to God's Word, you are poor. Relational peace with God brings freedom from debilitating sin and envy. How many rich people do you know who are debilitated by alcoholism, drugs, lust, or greed? They're not wealthy. They may be rich, but they're not wealthy. Wealth begins in personal peace with God.

2) **Real wealth includes relationship.**
   What resources do you have in your natural family? What resources do you have in your spiritual yoke partners, those with whom you have fellowship in God? What resources do you have in your friends and your community? Nothing is more tragic than the man whose only friend is his wallet: He is a man who will go to his grave lonely, isolated, or perhaps feared, but neither loved nor respected. Building, nurturing, and cherishing relationships with other people is part of real wealth, and it is an essential part of building up ALMIGHTY & SONS.

3) **Real wealth includes understanding your destiny and place in God's work and functioning accordingly.**

   Your skills, gifts, ministry, and spiritual growth are real wealth. This also includes the wisdom to avoid presumption and stay within your sphere.

   We could do a six hour conference on business expansion based on the law of discovering your sphere and staying inside it. Thousands of businessmen have done well in one sphere, gone into something else because it looked good and lost their shirts. Why? Because they didn't understand their boundaries. Only Christ has unlimited boundaries. The rest of us are circumscribed. Paul wrote, "We will not boast beyond our measure, but within the measure of the sphere which God apportioned to us..."[23] He refused to go outside his appointed sphere.

Do you believe that God has a purpose for everything He ordains? Of course. Did God ordain your business? If He didn't, you'd better find something else to do. But if He did, then He has a purpose for it. Have you ever spent time on your knees before God asking Him, "Why did you ordain my company?" If your business has a design, your job is to discover its design, find its sphere, and make sure that you do not expand outside it. Never mind all the conventional wisdom about vertical and horizontal integration. You need to find God's design for your business and stay inside it. God wants your business to do more than just create riches for you. He wants it to be a testimony in the Kingdom. You will need to learn the skills of strategic thinking to accomplish this. Find a mentor if you don't already have one. Pray them into your life.

4) **Real wealth includes good health, which means time to fulfill your destiny.**

It doesn't matter how good your ideas are, or how much treasure you have. If you don't have *time* to put them to work, you are bankrupt. The older we get, the more we understand the psalmist when he prays, "So teach us to number our days, that we may present to Thee a heart of wisdom."[24]

5) **Real wealth includes material contentment.**

In 1 Timothy 6:6-10, Paul acknowledges that we need sufficient possessions to carry out our calling. In some

---

[23] 2 Cor. 10:13
[24] Psa. 90:12

cases this means mere food and covering (verse 8).
In other cases, it may mean millions of dollars. In
any case, if we have enough to carry out our calling,
we should be content.

## Your Calling Determines Your Need for Money

Why do some people need more money than others? Because their
calling requires it. The tragedy in Christianity is that Christians, to
whom God has given money, usually do not use it for the sake of their
calling. They seldom discern their calling, so they seldom apply the
wealth God gives them, including riches, to that calling. We need to
understand what our calling is, and our calling is intimately tied up
with our resource base.

If you seem to be smitten with a huge bank account, don't count
that just as God's personal blessing to be lavished on yourself. It's a
clue regarding your calling. Ask the Lord, "Why do I have these
resources, and what am I supposed to do with them?" Capital that is
not directed to the call of God is one of the greatest snares anyone can
ever touch. That's why Paul says,

> Instruct those who are rich in this present
> world not to be conceited or to fix their hope
> on the uncertainty of riches, but on God, who
> richly supplies us with all things to enjoy.
> Instruct them to do good, to be rich in good
> works, to be generous and ready to share,
> storing up for themselves the treasure of a
> good foundation for the future, so that they
> may take hold of that which is life indeed.[25]

The Old Testament concludes with both a promise and the
warning of a curse:

> Remember the law of Moses My servant, even
> the statutes and ordinances which I commanded
> him in Horeb for all Israel. Behold, I am going

---

[25] 1 Tim. 6:17-19

> to send you Elijah the prophet before the
> coming of the great and terrible day of the
> Lord. And he will restore the hearts of the
> fathers to their children, and the hearts of
> the children to their fathers, lest I come
> and smite the land with a curse.
>
> *Mal. 4:4-6*

How much clearer can it be said? Ministries which bridge and bind the generations of fathers' hearts to their children bring forth blessing. Single generational thinking produces a curse. We're now under that curse, and it must go. May God grant us the wisdom, and riches wisely spent, to blow that curse into Hell.

At some point in time, it would be helpful to discuss at length some of the significant differences between family-owned/family-run businesses and the large corporation model. While not saying that the corporate model is necessarily unbiblical, despite its successes it brings with it a host of potentially complicating challenges. Suffice it to say, there is a reason that the majority of business-related G.N.P. comes from smaller, tightly-held businesses.

# CHAPTER FOUR

# Our God Loves to Work

*"But He answered them, 'My Father is working until now, and I Myself am working.'"*
John 5:17

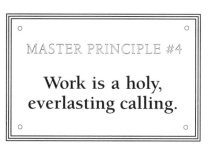

MASTER PRINCIPLE #4

**Work is a holy, everlasting calling.**

Work is not part of the curse. It preceded sin and the fall of man, and Jesus taught that work is eternal.[1] Heaven is no retirement village in the sky. It is where God's work is done more efficiently because sin is gone. Removing sin from work is like removing sand from the gears of a transmission. Everything goes more smoothly. While we only have a hint in scripture about the kind of work we will do in the future, be sure of one thing—you will be working. Wherever God is, there is work. It is a holy, everlasting calling, and He loves to do it.

Let's hear Jesus speak to us about work:

> But He answered them, "My Father is working until now, and I myself am working." For this cause therefore the Jews were seeking all the more to kill Him, because He not only was breaking the Sabbath, but also was calling God His own Father, making Himself equal with God. Jesus therefore answered and was saying to them, "Truly, truly, I say to you, the Son can do nothing of Himself, unless it is something He sees the Father doing; for whatever the Father does, these things the Son also does in like manner. For the Father loves the Son, and shows Him all things that He Himself is doing; and greater works than these will He show Him, that you may marvel." *John 5:17-20*

---

[1]John 5:17-20

Here's a cosmic good news/bad news joke: The good news is, Heaven really does exist, but the bad news is that it isn't the "ultimate weekend." It's a sin-free work environment! As Jesus tells us in John's gospel, when you study the Father, He shows you where and how He is working. God is an incredibly active Creator, and that is the understatement of this book.

## Meet God the Worker

God first reveals Himself in Genesis as a Creator, Worker, and Entrepreneur. He takes life, law, and energy out of His own Spirit-self and puts it into the material Cosmos He creates. The Greek word "Cosmos," which we translate "world," literally has as part of its meaning the inherent need to "tend or care for the thing that is created." It could be translated, "creation to-be-cared-for," in terms of its conceptual meaning. Strong's Concordance notes that the word "world" (Cosmos) derives its meaning from the Greek word, "Comizo," which means to take care of.[2] The Greek word in the New Testament translated, "Earth," comes from a totally separate word, "ge," which means soil or ground.[3] The Greek word used for Father's work in John 5 is, "ergazomai," which is to be engaged with or minister to.[4] The Earth is dirt and will pass away and be transformed, but the created Cosmos, which encompasses the Earth but is greater than the Earth, will eternally be tended by ALMIGHTY & SONS. It will always engage us in the privilege of caring for it. What began in the Garden of Eden will extend to the whole Earth.

We see the working nature of God all the way into the next age. In Revelation 21:10 we see the Church coming down to her earthly abode out of the heavens with Christ in her center, ruling over and from the Earth. Remember this is after the "Millennium" of Revelation 20 and

---

[2] *Strong's Greek Dictionary of the New Testament*; language section — "Greek" p. 43
[3] Ibid p. 20
[4] Ibid p. 32

the Great White Throne judgment. Revelation 22:1-2 is an especially intriguing verse:

> And he showed me a river of the water of life,
> clear as crystal, coming from the throne of God
> and of the Lamb, in the middle of its street. And
> on either side of the river was the tree of life,
> bearing twelve kinds of fruit, yielding its fruit
> every month; and the leaves of the tree were
> for the healing of the nations.

Please take note of two facts: (1) Nations will still exist in the next age, and (2) they will still need healing. The rest of this final chapter uses words like "serve" (vs. 3) and "reign" (vs. 5) which means to actively rule over and to administrate. There is no mention of rocking chairs or linen hammocks. The overcomer's reward is the rulership of nations.[5] Still want to go to Heaven?  Let's all agree that the other place has torment, which means they're still trying to accomplish things, but with no possibility of communication or success. Some of us feel like we've already worked a little in that environment and want no part of it!

The promise of a work-free Heaven is a heresy and reveals also a lack of biblical scholarship and knowledge of God. Work is the incarnation of my intangible "soul" out into God's universe. This is a very deep truth and worthy of a major effort to more fully draw it out. Work allows what is inside me to be revealed in the outside world. That is why God created the concept of work and loves it so much, because what is inside God is so spectacular it must be externally revealed. It is through His work that we see who He is! What an incredible and revealing thing work really is once we understand it from a biblical  point of view. No wonder so many people hate work: It reveals externally what is inside of them, and that isn't very pretty.

---

[5] Rev. 2:26-27

## Our Work Reveals Our Soul

James picks up this truth as he writes to us:

> What is the source of quarrels and conflicts
> among you? Is not the source your pleasures
> that wage war in your members? You lust and
> do not have; so you commit murder. And you
> are envious and cannot obtain; so you fight
> and quarrel. You do not have because you do
> not ask. You ask and do not receive, because
> you ask with wrong motives, so that you may
> spend it on your pleasures.     *James. 4:1-3*

Among other issues, James is telling us that external confusion and strife are nothing more than external revelation of sin within us. What is in me does come out of me and shows up in my attitudes and commitment to excellence (or lack thereof) in my work. Who do you suppose sees the "real you" most clearly—your pastor or your boss? One you are with only several hours a week, and then only when you're on your best behavior. The other you're with eight hours a day, when you're feeling good, bad, or ugly. That is why, in terms of economic evangelism, if we could get Christian managers to see that they're really *pastors in the marketplace*, we'd have a revival! I'll say more about this later. Suffice to say, your work reveals your soul. Work is how the soul is revealed and becomes visible.

The economic implications of this truth are massive in terms of how they affect a company's work force or even that of a whole nation. The pastoral and relational implications are equally significant as the more pragmatic issues like quality control and competitive edges are brought into focus. Let me give you a clear example out of my own experience.

Some years ago I wanted to buy a new car. I wanted to buy an American car as a point of national support, but I also wanted to buy a car that would serve me and my family as a point of safety, economic quality, and economy. I went to a trusted brother in the Lord who had sold cars for many years and shared my concerns, and

I asked for his advice. What he shared with me was an eye-opener that illustrates our point precisely.

He said, "Dennis, let me ask you a question. Would you rather buy an automobile from a company where labor and management live in a strongly adversarial relationship, with workers focusing on their 'rights' and an 'I don't get paid to do this' attitude? Or would you rather buy an automobile where labor and management are mutually supportive with one common goal of making the highest quality car on the market for the best competitive price?" What could I say? Sold, Toyota. And by the way, thirteen years and 180,000 miles later I know I made the right choice.

The point is this: Our labor reflects our motives, attitudes, goals, and the internal and external harmony of our environment. Economics is much more about people's souls than studying curves, charts, and computer analysis printouts of currency and stock market trends. Those measure results more than causes. And trade deficits say more about work ethics than protectionist legislation. God knows about all this since He invented the whole possibility of work-soul transfer. By the way, can you imagine the kind of art, music, and communication that await us in the sin-free age to come, where people's souls are freely and creatively released? Sign me up all over again, Jesus!

## Where Are the Christian Craftsmen?

Where are the craftsmen? Where is the work ethic? They're buried under the sick American soul. What will it take for America to learn that taking the Christian influence out of our national public life is a catastrophic *economic* choice as much as anything else. In the nonsensical and unconstitutional act of excluding values from the public realm under the guise of the separation of "church from state," we're really torpedoing America's economic future. Spiritual values show up quickly in our labor. Ideas have consequences, and of all the world's major religions, *only Christianity has a theology of labor.* Why? It's because work is a holy everlasting calling, and God loves to work. His soul lives to be incarnated.

In order to get millions of the Church's tradesmen and business professionals, who make up the world's work force, totally free, we must strike a deathblow to the second-class view of work in the real world. We must convince them that they aren't carnal, and God loves them and honors them not one bit less than those who have earned a living from the ministry in the local church. Christian workers of the world unite: You have nothing to lose but your false theology, and everything to gain in your new found mission!

Here is one more significant point before we shift gears. God, the Worker, absolutely hates unemployment. In Matthew 20:1-15, we see Jesus make this point with amazing clarity in the parable of the landowner. Because most of us in the Western world have been raised in a socialist culture, we relate to this passage from the point of view of the laborers and the apparent "injustice" of their equal pay for unequal work. However, what Jesus says is that our socialist attitudes reveal more about our problems with *envy* than with justice (vs. 15). The heart of the parable is the landowner's deep agitation over unhired men hanging out, wasting their lives in the marketplace. At least four times he went out looking for unhired men. Not once is his concern for profit or even the fruit of his personal vineyard ever mentioned. He has one supreme concern: unhired lives, that is, men and women "rotting" in life.

God hates to see people without a job. Our modern solution, rather than unshackling our economy, is to pay out welfare. I say this: To pay someone not to work robs him or her of their dignity and helps destroy their soul. God the Work-lover sees these unused gifts and the tragedy of people's helplessness and dependency on other men, and sees indignity instead of aid. No wonder the fish (the unsaved) are biting on economic issues and hammering on the issues of employment. Could it be that they see something that we Christians haven't seen yet about the work/dignity relationship?

## Work Produces Both Wealth and Riches

As mentioned in chapter three, there is a major difference in what our labors can produce and what Christ says we should *seek* out of our labors. Perhaps the best way to further explore this subject is to ask the question, "Are wealth and riches wrong?"

Many people quote 2 Corinthians chapter 8 verse 9: "...though He was rich, yet for your sakes He became poor." That's interpreted, "Well, Jesus was poor, so to follow Him we must be poor, too." But Jesus became poor for a reason: "...for your sakes He became poor, that you through His poverty might become rich." Since the context discusses our spiritual need, not our material condition, the passage does not say that Christ came to make us materially rich. But neither does it imply that we should be materially poor. Instead, in 2 Corinthians chapters 8 and 9, Paul explains that he wants Christians to imitate Christ by pouring themselves out in service to others so that they, too, may come to know and enjoy God in all His goodness.

In Matthew 6:19-20, Jesus said this:

> Do not lay up for yourselves treasures on
> earth, where moth and rust destroy and
> where thieves break in and steal; but lay
> up for yourselves treasures in heaven,
> where neither moth nor rust destroys and
> where thieves do not break in and steal.
> For where your treasure is, their your
> heart will be also.

Again, many Christians misconstrue these verses. They think God doesn't want us to prosper. But Christ didn't mean that at all. If He had, He would have nullified the covenant of Deuteronomy 8:18: "But you shall remember the Lord your God, for it is He who is giving you power to make wealth, that He may confirm His covenant which He swore to your fathers, as it is this day." Jesus never nullified the Old Covenant; instead, He fulfilled it and affirmed its validity as long as Heaven and Earth abide.[6] Paul drives home the point: "For all the promises of God in Him are 'Yes,' and in Him 'Amen,' to the glory of God through us."[7] If anything, the promises of God's covenant with

---

[6] Matt. 5:17-20
[7] 2 Cor. 1:20

Abraham, reiterated to Israel, are intensified to the Church under the New Covenant.

The power to create wealth is one of God's gifts under the covenant. Far from nullifying God's covenantal gift of the ability to create wealth, the New Covenant under Christ intensifies it. Christians who live faithfully under the covenant should be even more effective at creating wealth than believers under the Old Covenant.

Why, then, did Jesus say, "Do not lay up for yourselves treasures upon earth... but lay up for yourselves treasures in heaven" (Matt. 6:19-20). He said it to distinguish worldly riches—or what we'll call simply riches—from wealth. The Bible doesn't distinguish the two by these words, but it does by context. Riches are material; wealth is spiritual. Riches burn up in the fire of judgment; wealth passes through the fire.

Wealth is the product of stewarding for God the gifts He has given. Notice that in the parable of the minas the challenge to be obedient to God was to steward what God had given. The nobleman, representing Jesus, did not commission anybody to go out and win souls.[8] He commissioned people to take what God the Creator had invested in them and increase it.

If you will steward and increase the gifts God has given you, people will get saved around you because you will radiate what God created you to do and be, and they will experience life. If you want people to get saved, don't just hand out tracts. Hand out a life that you have stewarded to God's delight.

## Kingdom Economics Is Wealth Oriented

Why can't we read the Bible clearly? Why doesn't its message get into our brains? It's there, sure enough. Jesus said, if we may paraphrase Him, "Here's what I want you to do: Steward the gifts! And when I come back, I will reward you by making you rulers of cities." When

---

[8] Luke 19:12-26

Jesus spoke of the nobleman's return, which represents His own return, He made it clear that cities will have new rulers: faithful Christians who have stewarded His gifts fruitfully.

Wealth is made up of the ability and character skills that we gain to manage the material world. As already seen, riches, in contrast, are primarily material goods that one can gain with or without obedience to God. You do not have to obey God to become rich. Many people become rich through crime, exploitation, and pure lust for worldly goods. Wealth may produce riches, but riches cannot produce wealth because wealth comes from obedience to the covenant.

We talked about this in chapter three in looking at 1 Corinthians 3:10-15 which says that all our work will be tested by fire. The work that has produced wealth will pass through death; the work that has not produced wealth will end with death. Don't worry about trying to produce a lot of riches, but give yourself to the production of wealth, character, and godly stewardship. If you do that, *riches will take care of themselves.* We need billions of dollars for the work of the Kingdom; go produce your share. But go knowing that the game is not really about money; it is about developing love, skill, obedience, and knowledge.

When we move away from capitalism, which is riches oriented, to Kingdom economics, which is wealth oriented, stewardship replaces riches as our motivation. When that happens, contentment replaces envy, greed, and discontent. Godly strategic planning produces contentment, with or without riches, because it produces the lasting fruit of wealth. If you're like me, you've known some very rich people who were not content. They had riches, but they were never satisfied; they were always scrounging for more. Why? It's because they were trying to get the satisfaction from riches that is only possible through wealth. Like a man in a lifeboat who in desperation drinks saltwater to quench his thirst, they find that the more they consume the more madly they crave it.

Solomon knew their lot. His great purpose in Proverbs and Ecclesiastes was to help people see that laying up treasures on Earth is vanity:

> Thus I hated all the fruit of my labor for which
> I had labored under the sun, for I must leave it
> to the man who will come after me. And who
> knows whether he will be a wise man or a fool?
> Yet he will have control over all the fruit of my
> labor for which I have labored by acting wisely
> under the sun. This too is vanity. Therefore I
> completely despaired of all the fruit of my labor
> for which I had labored under the sun. When
> there is a man who has labored with wisdom,
> knowledge, and skill, then he gives his legacy to
> one who has not labored with them. This too is
> vanity and a great evil.          *Eccl. 2:18-21*

Solomon's problem was that he was a poor father. Because he did not raise his sons to be godly, Solomon's own sons split the kingdom, and everything for which he labored was destroyed. Remember a major principle of chapter three: Wise stewardship over property operates generationally rather than short-run. God wants us to transmit real wealth to our children, and real wealth is the power to do God's will on Earth as it is done in Heaven.

### God Is Calling for Christian Revival through the Work Place

I have sometimes been tempted to start a "hire the heathen club" after being burned by Christian workers. I wonder how many of you, out of your own experience with slipshod, presumptuous Christian work, would want to join my club? Obviously my sarcasm poorly conceals a lot of pain. This ought not to be, since Christians ought to be the best workers on the planet because their Father is so vested in excellent work.

As we have seen, far too many Christians think work is a part of the curse, so they never really put their hearts into it. Christian employers have been burned by lazy Christians, so heavenly minded they're no earthly good. Christian employers have typically aggravated the problem by taking it easy on them "because they are brothers." And my experience has shown me that much of the world thinks Christian employees are not necessarily a bargain either.

## Let's Turn Up the Heat for Christian Excellence

The opposite should be true. If you have a Christian employee, you should require more from him than if he were unsaved! When you hire him, you should tell him right up front: "I'm going to require more from you, not less, because you're a believer. If you don't measure up, I'll terminate you faster than I would if you were unsaved, because Jesus said in Luke 12:48, 'And from everyone who has been given much shall much be required; and to whom they entrusted much, of him they will ask all the more.' That's how God operates."

For years deterioration in both the quality and the quantity of work has occurred in much of the United States. The solution begins with Christians renouncing and repenting from their anti-work attitudes. We have stripped our culture of the Reformed work ethic that lies at the root of the economic productivity of the industrialized world. Probably most of the American people now view work as a curse. Getting to the weekend and the material things they desire (not personal fulfillment through their work) is the goal of their labor. We won't see a fundamental change in our economy until the Church repents of its anti-work attitude and views work as a blessed call to which Christians commit themselves just as God does.

Once we see this truth with sufficient clarity to communicate it, we will be ready to begin to transform the other organizations that have come together around the business community. If we can revive the biblical work ethic, we will begin an economic turnaround wherever clear thinking Christians labor. Our grandchildren, should the Lord tarry, will rise up and call us blessed, and so will the Chamber of Commerce, unsaved though it may be.

Ultimately, economic collapse or not, we believers will still need to get our work ethic cleaned up—whether here on Earth or in eternity. Work is a holy, everlasting calling, and Almighty will get His passion for self-fulfilling labor into His sons and daughters as surely as He is God, even if it takes forever.

# CHAPTER FIVE

# The Product of the Family Business Is Service

*"The kings of the Gentiles lord it over them; and those who have authority over them are called 'Benefactors.' But not so with you, but let him who is the greatest among you become as the youngest, and the leader as the servant. For who is greater, the one who reclines at the table, or the one who serves? Is it not the one who reclines at the table? But I am among you as the one who serves."*
Luke 22:25-27

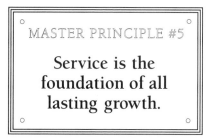

MASTER PRINCIPLE #5

**Service is the foundation of all lasting growth.**

*I*t is my goal to help you not only to become a fruitful partner in ALMIGHTY & SONS yourself, but also to help you multiply yourself by *helping others* to become fruitful partners as well. What will it take for you to do that?

You'll have to become a more effective servant. Our goal must be God's goal and that is to be involved in enabling others to become proprietors. Servant leaders produce a spirit of proprietorial ownership in others.

This is the heart of the difference between someone (Christian or non-Christian) who builds his business on Christian principles, and someone who doesn't. The latter is satisfied to get employees who make him rich. The former is satisfied only if he can produce *new proprietors who become partners in the business and prosper in it themselves.* In other words, Christian leaders are committed to making others wealthy, not rich.

## True Leaders Produce Fellow Workers

I continue to stress that our goal is not to make a profit or gain employees; the goal is to make partners and proprietors. This is the pattern God sets for us. Multiplying proprietors is the focus; profit is the by-product. When people are born again, they become "children of God, and if children, then heirs, heirs of God and joint heirs with Christ."[1]

God's aim is not that we should remain mere employees for eternity, but that we should become members of the family and partners in His business. We're junior partners, to be sure, but partners all the same. That is why Christ said this to His disciples in John 15:15-16: "No longer do I call you slaves; for the slave does not know what his master is doing; but I have called you friends, for all things that I have heard from My Father I have made known to you. You did not choose Me, but I chose you, and appointed you, that you should go and bear fruit..." It is also why He challenged His disciples with this question in Luke 16:12: "...if you have not been faithful in what is another man's, who will give you what is your own?"

Anybody can find an employee who will work for him, as long as he offers a high enough wage. That employer is merely buying his employee's work. But employees are not what the Christian business vision is all about. It is about partners, associates, and proprietors. It is about people who have a stake in the business that goes beyond their weekly paycheck. It is about transforming people from employees to co-owners, from orphans to heirs.

One businessman who exemplifies this vision was Sam Walton, founder of Wal-Mart Stores. Wal-Mart grew in thirty years from an obscure five-and-dime store in Bentonville, Arkansas, to America's largest discount retail chain, with nearly two thousand stores and $44 billion in sales by the end of 1991. "Mr. Sam," as he encouraged everyone in the company to call him, became the country's richest man, not only by insisting that his stores always give shoppers low prices on all items, but also by ensuring that all his workers had a direct personal stake in the company's performance. He didn't call them employees; he called them *associates.*

In addition to cash wages and insurance benefits, every Wal-Mart associate also receives stock in the company. As a result, even though most earn less in hourly pay or annual salary than workers

---

[1] Rom. 8:16-17 (KJV)

with similar jobs at other companies, they are fiercely loyal to the company, knowing that its success promises them considerable wealth in the long-run as a reward for their sacrifices in the short-run. When Walton died, *The Wall Street Journal* reported:

> Although Wal-Mart executives typically earn less salary than their peers at other big retailers, and work longer hours, the stock plan created by Mr. Walton has made many of them rich. [Chief Executive Officer] David Glass, for example, had a fiscal 1990 salary of $630,000. That's under the earnings of the chief executives of two smaller retailers: the $898,928 for Joseph Antonini of Kmart and the $1.4 million for Kenneth Macke of Dayton Hudson [Target Store parent company]. But Mr. Glass leaves them behind when stock option and employee-stock-ownership plans are included. His Wal-Mart stock, obtained largely through options, is worth nearly $80 million.

> And the stock plans don't benefit only top executives. Many rank and file workers have done well on Wal-Mart stock. After nearly 25 years at the company, Shirley Cox, a cashier, still earned barely $7 an hour. But she retired in her 40's on $250,000 of company stock...

> "The stock is a prevailing theme for everyone at Wal-Mart," says the 25-year-old assistant manager of a store in the Kansas City area who works more than 50 hours a week but earns less than $25,000 a year. "There's sort of a promise that if you hang around long enough, you can make a fortune on the stock."[2]

Walton's vision for giving every worker a stake in the company is part of the reason why, after the founder's death, most analysts remained confident that the company would continue its phenomenal

---

[2] *The Wall Street Journal,* April 6, 1992, pp. A1, A6

20 percent annual growth for years to come. It could be pointed out, however, that Wal-Mart might have been even more effectively structured had it franchised its leveraged position and promoted individual ownership rather than collective ownership .

We dwell on Walton's story because it so clearly illustrates three fundamental principles about the Christian vision of business leadership. First, "Mr. Sam" considered himself his workers' servant. He didn't lord his authority over them. On any given day, he might show up unannounced at any store and throw himself into any task, from greeting customers at the door to gathering carts in the parking lot. Second, he understood that advancement must follow on faithfulness, that whoever is faithful in little will be faithful in much. For that reason, very few Wal-Mart managers or executives are ever imported from outside the company; almost all rise through the ranks. Third, he ensured that faithful workers became part owners of the company, thus tying their rewards to their performance.

A short-term, profit-oriented vision can be satisfied merely by gaining employees. A long-term, servant-oriented vision strives instead to facilitate other people becoming proprietors themselves. The best way to make a business profitable is to have as many proprietors and as few employees as possible, because proprietors generate maximum profit. Why? Because they work harder, longer, and smarter out of a sense of ownership and involvement. That's why profit sharing works. To put it simply, people naturally care more about what belongs to them than they do about what belongs to someone else. Here's the real question: How are you going to implement these truths with those you lead or influence?

## What Is a True Servant Leader?

Most Christians are familiar with Christ's saying that whoever wants to be great in the Kingdom of Heaven must learn to be the servant of all. Few, however, have a biblical understanding of what real servant leadership is. All too common is the notion that servant leaders do everything for everybody. But doing everything for someone would merely make that person lazy and dependent. Real servant leaders follow Christ's example. He serves His people by enabling them to fulfill their own destiny in God's plan.

This is true at the fundamental level of salvation and sanctification. We contribute nothing to our regeneration. God finds us "dead in... trespasses and sins" and unilaterally makes "us alive together with Christ (by grace you have been saved)."[3] Then God continues His good work in us, transforming us into fruitful children. Paul says in Ephesians 2:8-10: "For by grace you have been saved through faith, and that not of yourselves, it is the gift of God; not as a result of works, that no one should boast. For we are His workmanship, created in Christ Jesus for good works, which God prepared beforehand, that we should walk in them." God sanctifies us and empowers us to do these good works as Paul made clear when he wrote, "...work out your salvation with fear and trembling; for it is God who is at work in you, both to will and to work for His good pleasure."[4] And what is His pleasure in us? Paul made that clear, too, when he wrote this:

> And we know that God causes all things to work together for good to those who love God, to those who are called according to His purpose. For whom He foreknew, He also predestined to become conformed to the image of His Son, that He might be the first-born among many brethren; and whom He predestined, these He also called; and whom He called, these He also justified; and whom He justified, these He also glorified.
>
> *Rom. 8:28-30*

God has planned a destiny for every one of His children, and He works in us to achieve that destiny.

The Bible speaks of our destiny, the purpose for which God made us, not only in terms of eternity and Heaven, salvation, sanctification, and glorification, but also in terms of time and this world. God gives everyone gifts suitable for particular service, whether in the Church,[5]

---

[3] Eph. 2:1,5
[4] Phil. 2:12-13
[5] Rom. 12:3-8; 1 Cor. 12:6-11

or in the world, for it is God who put wisdom even in the hearts of all the gifted artisans.[6] He gives people gifts, not to serve themselves, but to serve others.[7]

The single greatest motivator people can have is to see that God handcrafted them and therefore they have a design. Parents, business leaders, pastors, and all who lead must help people to discover their design and fulfill their destiny in God. The godly servant leader has one primary goal: to draw others into their full potential in God. That, friend, is the work and definition of a true servant leader.

### Good Leaders Gradually Share More and More Responsibility

If we are to build strong families, strong churches, or strong businesses, then we, like our Heavenly Father, must share authority and responsibility incrementally with those we lead. We must draw them into partnership with us, giving them increasing amounts of responsibility according to their calling, ability, and faithfulness. Your primary job in your business is to help those who work with you to discover what they are supposed to do in your business, and to draw their skills out so they can do their work better and more effectively.

This implies an ethic for business that is not profit driven but servant driven. But it is precisely this sort of business that will also, in the long-run, be most profitable. When all the people in an organization are doing what they are designed to do, they will be not only happy and fulfilled, but also very productive. We are not to seek the profit as an end in itself; we are to seek to serve those with whom we work. Profit is a fruit, not a goal. Whoever serves best will also accumulate an eternal wealth of character.

The converse is also true. If people are not supposed to be in your business, you need to steer them out of it. Never let a false sense of compassion drive you to retain a worker whom God has not called

---

[6] Ex. 31:6
[7] Eph. 4:11-16

and gifted for your business. If the work is contrary to his or her motivation and skills, the kindest thing you can do is to help them find a job where they do fit. Nothing can prosper in the long-run by operating against its inherent design. You can force people into situations for utilitarian purposes in the short-run, but in the long-run anybody operating against their design will lose money, cause problems to the organization, and promote sin, because whatever is out of order is not of God and cannot prosper.

Do you want to be involved evangelistically in the business community? Try concentrating less on giving workers gospel tracts and more on helping them to discover and develop the design and potential God wrought in them. It's tough work. It requires time and close attention. As Solomon put it in Proverbs 20:5 (KJV), "Counsel in the heart of man is like deep water; but a man of understanding will draw it out." Chances are they've never had a father who did that. Some may have never even had a pastor who did that. They've never known anyone who helped them discover their design. But that is what Christian business leaders and professionals are to do, and when we do it we'll find workers not only grateful that someone truly shows an interest in them, but also excited about what God can do in and through them. Openness to the gospel follows true service. What better place to express this than in the marketplace!

## Sacrifice Is the Source of Expansion

In Matthew 10:39, Jesus invites us to come to Him and die. Seldom is this message preached in places preoccupied with popularity and growth. This is not a "user friendly" church sermon: "He who has found his life shall lose it, and he who has lost his life for My sake shall find it." Oh joy! I get to die. Some heartwarming message. The problem is, it's true. It is in dying to my own agenda and taking on God's agenda that I become fruitful and multiply. It is a principle of God's Cosmos that selfishness begets death, isolation, and poverty, whereas spending our lives on others is the source of life, fellowship, and multiplication.

Again the Master Economist and Manager said it perfectly: "Truly, truly, I say to you, unless a grain of wheat falls into the earth and dies, it remains by itself alone; but if it dies, it bears much fruit" (John 12:24). Growth is fueled by sacrifice. '

So does God expect us to become self-flagellating monks who work tirelessly with no breaks, giving all we have to the poor? No. The sacrifice we're dealing with here is a sacrifice of another kind.

## Understanding the Hidden Life of the Leader

Paul exhorts us in Colossians 3:23, "Whatever you do, do your work heartily, as for the Lord rather than for men." In Matthew 6:1-18, Christ spends significant time reiterating the same principle. If we live and act to be seen of men, then our reward is paid by men, not by God. God Himself openly rewards those who live *before Him* rather than those who are living before men and who are motivated by men's approval. Psalm 127:1 says, "Unless the Lord builds the house, they labor in vain who build it." The point is this: If we're in our right minds, we want God to do the building and to be the Senior Partner in what is being built, not us. And in order to do that, we must learn to hide. Hiding means getting underneath people and pushing them up.

## Why Are We after Owners Rather Than Employees?

Let me give a good working example which comes out of my own experience as a business owner and a manager for many years. There is a clear difference between an employee and an owner. The employee comes to work at 7:59 and 59 seconds. He punches the time clock and heads toward his work station. A catastrophe might be taking place somewhere else in the plant, but since he doesn't get paid to deal with that problem, the employee proceeds directly to his own work station. You have his body and his mind in the same place until about 9:45, but then his mind begins to leave his body in anticipation of the upcoming work break. After the break, his mind and body reconverge until about 11:40, when they separate once again in mental anticipation of the lunch break. The same thing happens just prior to the afternoon break and then finally, about one-half hour before he's off, the employee's mind leaves permanently. Punching the time clock at 5:00 sharp, he is "out of there," having done what he's paid to do, and secure that the boss didn't take advantage of any of "his rights." He has no further thought of his job; it doesn't exist until the next morning. Why should it? He is an employee. While this may be an exaggeration to many, it makes the point.

The owner or manager comes to work when the work load requires, but virtually always before the employee arrives, and he's there long after the employee. The owner picks up trash when he sees it, helps where he can, and has the opposite problem of the employee: He can't get his mind off his work, even when he's at home, problematic as this is.

What are the differences between the employee and the owner or manager? There are at least three: (1) Employees tend to focus on their rights whereas leaders focus on their responsibilities, (2) Leaders have a "piece of the action" in some proportional way, and (3) You don't make profit on employees; at best they help you break even. Profit is generated by the people with a proprietorial spirit.

To further illustrate where I am going with this, let me tell another story. Several years ago I attended a private gathering for high-powered Christian business leaders and chief executive officers. During the course of the conference, several Fortune 500 executives began to share what a tough year it had been for them personally. Their salaries were still high, into six figures, and their health and families well. The problem was that one of the C.E.O.'s had to lay off 18,000 employees, another 11,000, and yet another 6,000. The pain and anguish I heard in them was deep and life changing. Carrying that kind of responsibility for others takes its toll and should be properly, but not exorbitantly, rewarded.

If the blood of the martyrs is the growth of the Church, then the welfare of the people in the leader's heart is the engine of growth for a business or trade. "...Unless a grain of wheat falls into the earth and dies, it remains by itself alone."[8] Solitariness and non-growth is the result of the grain of wheat's refusal to die to its own life. It is still holding to its "rights." People and nations whose economic values are centered in rights, rather than in a sense of responsibility, are destined to mediocrity and stagnation. The pain of growth is in the inner death of the leaders, and no amount of prestige, salary, or perks can take away that cross if it is truly there. It is the leader's point of fellowship with Christ. Life and growth require death and sacrifice. This is a master law of economic increase, and it is every bit as real and operable as the law of supply and demand. It's voluntarily shouldered by servant-hearted leaders.

## Let's Stop Playing the Political Left/Right Game

Recognizing that we've hardly touched this subject, permit me to make one last comment before we move on. We, as Christians, are not called by God to justify the world system's economic order. I am not an apologist for either capitalism or socialism. The downfall of secular capitalism is this: It uses evolution as its philosophical base, justifying the "survival of the fittest." It tends to turn people into objects of production and pawns of salesmanship and consumption. Socialism's downside is altogether as bad: It is paternalistic and creates a bureaucratic civil structure that "cares for the people" as poor unenlightened children who need to be led to understand their true place in the dialectic of history. It promotes indolence, dependency, envy, and ultimately theft and misappropriation through confiscatory taxes.

My commitment is not to capitalism or socialism—but rather to the Kingdom of God and an economic order built upon scripture. That order rests on what Christ called the "greatest of the command-ments." Hear them afresh:

> "You shall love the Lord your God with all
> your heart, and with all your soul, and with

---

[8] John 12:24

all your mind." This is the great and foremost
commandment. And a second is like it, "You
shall love your neighbor as yourself." On
these two commandments depend the whole
Law and the Prophets.          *Matt. 22:37-40*

The summation of our economic order is found herein. It will
only work if it is led by servants whose hearts are set on seeing that
people are released into their destiny and that none are enslaved to
either the oppression of the tyrant, or the tyranny of the lazy and
indolent. For Christians the left/right game is a sucker's game we
shouldn't even consider. We're offering a third choice: the economics
of the Kingdom of God.

### True Economic Service Is Based on Obedience to God

Service is more than giving people what they want; it also involves
*not* giving them what God does not want them to have. Giving people
goods or services that support or cater to their fallen nature is not
serving them, and people or companies who do so will be among the
first to go under in tough times. If you really love me, tell me "no"
sometimes.

The heart of what we could share here goes beyond this study.
What needs to be said here is this: If you're really serving me and
mine, you won't offer goods or services that will cause me to
stumble.[9] In tough economic times, people who are offering true
value in their goods and services are the ones who will really prosper.

Businesses or services that cater to people's greed, vanity, lusts,
and the like are on the top of God's list for unemployment lines in the
coming economic crisis. While it is obvious that some people will
misuse or make a vice out of even good things, like clothing or food or
even recreational equipment, it is clear that there is a difference between
selling or trading in useless vanities, and providing legitimate services.
If there is a doubt, pray about it. Any honest inquiry before God will

---

[9] Rom. chapter 14

be answered in one way or another. And if you don't know if what you're doing is something God can bless, you can't do it in faith in any event. You must settle the issue, because to operate in unbelief about your work is sin.[10]

Those who serve most effectively will lead. It really is that simple. In any business or trade, in the long-run, the servants will succeed. The Almighty's business will succeed. It won't be because God is simply more powerful than Satan, but because God is a servant, and Satan is an exploiter. Even at the top, the servant always wins.

---

[10] "Whatsoever is not of faith is sin." Rom. 14:23

```
┌─────────────────────────────┐
│  ┌───────────────────────┐  │
│  │ ○                   ○ │  │
│  │                       │  │
│  │      SECTION          │  │
│  │       TWO             │  │
│  │ ○                   ○ │  │
│  └───────────────────────┘  │
└─────────────────────────────┘
```

# The Foundations Required to Build a Prosperous and Just Society

# CHAPTER SIX

# What Money Reveals about People

*"...for where your treasure is, there will your heart be also."*     Matt. 6:21

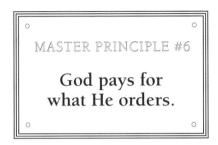

MASTER PRINCIPLE #6

**God pays for
what He orders.**

*D*o you believe that more money will solve most of your personal and business problems and bring you what you want? If so, you're wrong, and this chapter is the most important one in the book for you. In the next chapter, we will be dealing with the laws of sowing and reaping, but in this chapter, we'll see something equally important: Many of my limitations are designed by God to protect me.

The modern state operates from two major related economic deceptions: (1) virtually all problems are solved by throwing more money at them, and (2) if you run short of money, print more. Both ideas take us to the very core of fallen man's problem. He wants to be God, and he doesn't recognize the redemptive value of his own limitations.

This relationship between wanting to be God and worshipping money as the answer to all problems, is precisely why the Apostle Paul could say that, "the love of money is the root of all evil."[1] *God* is the answer to problems, not *money*; so why does fallen man worship money? Jesus gave us the answer when He said that what we treasure most reveals the love of our hearts.[2]

### Fallen Man Sees Money As the Ticket to Being a God

Let's review man's fall for a moment, since it bears directly on the issue at hand:

---

[1] 1 Tim. 6:10 (KJV)
[2] Matt. 6:21

Now the serpent was more crafty than
any beast of the field which the Lord God
had made. And he said to the woman,
"Indeed has God said, 'You shall not eat
from any tree of the garden?'"

And the woman said to the serpent,
"From the fruit of the trees of the garden
we may eat; but from the fruit of the
tree which is in the middle of the garden,
God has said, 'You shall not eat from it or
touch it, lest you die.'"

And the serpent said to the woman,
"You surely shall not die! For God knows
that in the day you eat from it your eyes
will be opened, and you will be like God,
knowing good and evil." When the woman
saw that the tree was good for food, and
that it was a delight to the eyes, and the
tree was desirable to make one wise, she
took from its fruit and ate; and she gave
also to her husband with her, and he ate.

*Gen. 3:1-6*

What principles are highlighted here?

1.  The temptation had to do with *limits*. Man was to
    respect God's limits for him and trust the Lord that
    these limits were for his own good and for his safety,
    rather than barriers to his growth and freedom, as
    Satan had asserted.

2.  Instead, man fell for the temptation because he saw
    in the Tree of the Knowledge of Good and Evil
    something that would give him the power to
    *supply his own needs* (food), give him power over
    himself and his environment (make him wise),
    and make him a god (knowing good and evil).

In other words, man would become independent of his Creator and God's imposed limits on him. Man could then use his own resources of self-acquired wisdom and self-acquired abilities to solve problems and create what he wanted. He would be a god, and what would be the ultimate goal of his power? The goal would be to use the power to get other men to do what he wanted them to do. And what would be the source of the power to make other men serve him and his wants, needs, and vision? Here's the answer: The source would be money. Money is a medium of exchange that will get those who serve him into the position of being gods as well; gods who in turn will get other men to serve them. Let's explain this further.

## Money and Power

Power over other men comes basically in only two ways. You can enslave them by brute force (and live in constant fear of them revolting against you), or you can pay them money to serve you. Obviously, the wise choice is to appeal to their own sense of self-interest rather than to enslave them. So, you choose money. It becomes your instrument of power, and in so doing, it becomes your ticket to being a god. It is then worshipped for what you believe it can do for you. It makes you "free." Small wonder loving money is the root of all evil; it violates God's first commandment by having another god, or source of life, besides the Lord. Whatever you make the primary source of power in your life becomes your god.

Before we follow up on these truths, let me share with you that this chapter is designed to reveal two major things about *you:* (1) how you view God's limits for yourself and your business, and whether you see those limits as a source of safety or a source of bondage; and (2) to give you further insight on the economic issues related to banking, debt, currency, and interest rates. The financial principles in this chapter form the very core of how to biblically manage your own finances, your business finances, and even those finances which run a nation's economy.

### "Money Problems" Are Usually a Symptom, Not the Root Problem

> Hear, O My people, and I will speak; O Israel,
> I will testify against you; I am God, your God.
> ...I shall take no young bull out of your house,
> nor male goats out of your folds. For every beast
> of the forest is Mine, the cattle on a thousand hills.
>
> *Psalm 50:7, 9-10*

> But our God is in the heavens; He does whatever
> He pleases.                                    *Psalm 115:3*

When you own not only the cattle on a thousand hills but also the hills themselves, you don't have a money problem. God, owning everything, has no resource needs. That doesn't mean that God is not a creative, diligent, master steward. He is, and He uses all those skills in His work. But be assured, *if God wants something done, He will pay for it.* You must understand this. *God pays for what He orders.*

### Understanding Why God Keeps Money from Us

God leads us by a number of different devices. Near the very top of the list of attention-getters are money problems. As you all know, money not only talks, sometimes it can shout! God not only uses money to reveal how much we look to Him as our ultimate source and problem solver, but He also uses it to teach us more about Himself and how He wants us to use better management skills. As I have said repeatedly, the goal of ALMIGHTY & SONS is to help people to be fruitful as they learn to manage according to "Father's way."

It took me years to be able to say that I fully believed this truth: "God pays for what He orders." I no longer believe in money problems. I do believe you can have problems with money, but since I began to realize how God uses money in our lives, it has changed my life. All future managers in Almighty's business can and will come to this same reality; it's that important.

When money appears to be the issue, I must remember Master Principle Number Six: "God pays for what He orders." He literally has all resources available to Him, so if He has not released as many of them to me as I think I need, then I must ask myself a series of questions. Even before I start down the list, I must also remember two more major truths: (1) I must thank God for His *limits on me* (withholding resources from me is one way of keeping me from destroying myself and others when I obviously don't see God's will yet), and (2) power is guarded by problems (the "money problem" I may now be experiencing is designed to reveal the *true nature* of problems I don't yet understand). Having said this, we're ready to proceed.

Let's go down a short list together of eight basic questions to ask ourselves when a lack of resources appears to be limiting our freedom, choices, or goals:

1. Is God keeping me from expansion or even from paying my current bills because of a particular moral sin in my life?

2. Is greed or materialism driving my desire for expansion? While God is not opposed to personal comfort, convenience, or things that make efficient use of our time and energy, He does oppose both greed and materialism.

3. Is this new project (or the one I have been following since I believe I last heard from God) in His perfect will for me or those associated with it? Do I care enough to fast and pray about this issue until I have an answer?

4. Is God trying to protect me from something or someone in this project? What is it, or who is it, and why? One of the root meanings of the Hebrew word "Shalom," which we translate "peace," is the ability to make wise covenants with people who will honor them. A lack of money is often a red light saying not only "stop," but also "identify the danger" that is around you.

5. Are you proceeding in this project God's way? Is there biblical truth you are in danger of transgressing? How diligent have you been in

searching God's Word for economic or management principles that might apply to this current problem?

6. If God doesn't supply the money when you want it, and in the form you want it, are you willing to take matters into your own hands? Would you get the money through unbiblical long-term loans or by cutting deals with people who by gut instinct you don't trust? Is your ambition stronger than your recognition of God's safety limits? If God ordered the project, could you really believe He'd pay for it biblically? Are you trying to play God and escape His limits?

7. Are you clear on the fact that God couldn't care less about your "money problem"?—instead, His concern is your "maturity problem." Has profit become a goal instead of a fruit for you? If simple profit is your goal, God may well resist you, since you are supposed to know better. As we have already seen, a Christian enterprise seeks to develop people and resources first, with profit following after.

8. Do you have enough management wealth and skill to properly steward this new expansion? If not, what skills or people will you need that you currently don't have? Remember, riches which exceed our management skills almost always ` severely damage us.

### Money Is Time in Foldable Form

Money is time in foldable form, that is, it is units of man's energy expended over time to secure or produce a particular service or product. To spend money is to spend your time and the time of others, and time is our most valuable asset.

This being the case, money has become a unique reminder to me of my limitations here on Earth. When I spend money, I am in effect saying that this is really what I want to do with the work units I spent producing this money. It represents the struggles, pressures, time spent away from my family, days closer to death, etc. Money really is very important in this sense: not so much as a means to acquire new things, but rather as a statement of how I value spending time already gone and invested.

As a Bible teacher for well over thirty years and one who carries pastoral responsibility for other men, it has amazed me how much my perspective changed as Christ began to take me into the realm of biblical economics and ALMIGHTY & SONS. The Word became alive and deep in new ways. Who would have thought that studying money, banking, and taxation policy, let alone management principles, would have led a preacher here? But it has, praise God! Early in this journey, Psalm 90 began to come alive to me as I began to ponder these truths about money. Let's look at several relevant verses:

> **Psalm 90:3-6**—Thou dost turn man back into dust. And dost say, "Return, O children of men." For a thousand years in Thy sight are like yesterday when it passes by, or as a watch in the night. Thou has swept them away like a flood, they fall asleep; in the morning they are like grass which sprouts anew. In the morning it flourishes, and sprouts anew; towards evening it fades, and withers away.

> **Psalm 90:12**—So teach us to number our days, that we may present to Thee a heart of wisdom.

> **Psalm 90:16-17**—Let Thy work appear to Thy servants, and Thy majesty to their children. And let the favor of the Lord our God be upon us; and do confirm for us the work of our hands; yes, confirm the work of our hands.

While there is much that could be said about these scriptures, let me share a point or two. Firstly, Moses sees the fleetingness of time and therefore the absolute necessity of learning how to measure it wisely and "number our days." Secondly, in verses 16 and 17 he petitions God to let His servants discern the true work of God, and what He is after, and to communicate the scope of its majestic nature to his offspring. He closes with a cry to "confirm the work of our hands," or put another way, "make sure that we are not wasting our time on issues or projects that are not really very important." Money can fool us, but if we see the true value of our time, it won't.

To discern the true nature of money is to begin to get in touch with meaningful living and life's real issues for you in your particular part of God's work. After all, what could be more discouraging than to die and find out that on Earth you wasted much of your time. Knowing this, as I now look at money, I am reminded of the units of time behind it and the call to steward it wisely. Spending money is spending time and establishing priorities.

## God Pays for What He Orders

The mature Christian steward, like the wise financial manager, doesn't fall into the trap of treating money as the solution to every problem. He sees it only as a tool, and he always understands that God's work, done in God's way, will never lack God's funding because God pays for what He orders. Hence, he can respect and use money, but he will never love it, never see it as an end in itself. He will neither be so hungry for money that he will willingly sell his future and freedom for it (like the incessant borrower who becomes the lender's slave),[3] nor be so afraid to use it as to avoid it altogether (like the wicked, lazy, unprofitable servant in the parables of the talents and minas).[4] Instead, like the wise servants in the parables, he will invest it wisely to produce a profit for ALMIGHTY & SONS.[5] Consequently, he will receive responsibilities and honor in the Kingdom.

---

[3] Prov. 22:7
[4] Matt. 25:24-30; Luke 19:20-27
[5] Matt. 25:16-23; Luke 19:16-19

## To Resist God's Limits Is to Find Fault with God

> But we will not boast beyond our measure,
> but within the measure of the sphere which
> God apportioned to us as a measure, to reach
> even as far as you. For we are not over-
> extending ourselves, as if we did not reach to
> you, for we were the first to come even as far
> as you in the gospel of Christ; not boasting
> beyond our measure, that is, in other men's
> labors, but with the hope that as your faith
> grows, we shall be, within our sphere, enlarged
> even more by you...                 *2 Cor. 10:13-15*

To go outside of our appointed sphere or limits is rebellion against God. It is, in effect, a statement that you are God and reserve the right to find fault with God's plans, substituting your own in their place. Money issues, for all the reasons we have seen, bring forth rebellion, if indeed it is there. To circumvent God's limits is simple rebellion, whether we see it or not, and God has a way of "helping" us to see it!

## Inflation Is Theft

A great temptation for those who idolize money is to rebel against limitedness and ignore God by seeing more money as the solution to all problems: to create more money out of nothing. Idolatrous governments expand the money supply without expanding the supply of the other elements in the economy. Consequently, the laws of supply and demand force down the value of all the money, old and new alike. In other words, prices of all other goods and services (enumerated in money) rise, while the value of money (enumerated in all other goods and services) falls. Such artificial expansion of the money supply is inflation, and the rising prices caused by it constitute price inflation.

Remember, money is the time value associated with the use and development of land, labor, capital, and products (goods and services) in foldable form. If you increase the supply of money without an equivalent increase in the supply of what it represents, the new money represents nothing and so has no value. For it to acquire value, it must steal value from old money. As a result, both the old money and the new will have lower value relative to the land, labor, capital, and goods and services they represent. Planned inflation is, in fact, theft. To attempt to circumvent God's provisions and create independently from God not only violates God's law, it illegally takes something away from someone else.

While it is beyond our purposes in this book to get deeply into the issue of debt and what the Bible says about it, it is obviously closely related to the issues of limits, presumption, and obedience.

## A Quick Look at Debt

Consumer debt may satisfy our wants in the short-run, but it is destructive in the long-run. The Bible does not forbid all debt (Leviticus 25), but it does call debt for consumption, "bondage." You may borrow to meet immediate needs, but by doing so you enslave yourself. Taking on debt doesn't set you free from want; it enslaves you to your creditor.[6] Furthermore, although Old Testament Law permitted the giving of property-secured loans to people in desperate need, with terms up to fifty years (Leviticus 25), it prohibited collecting on those loans during the sabbatical year.[7] This meant that after every sixth year, creditors would have to wait for a whole year before receiving another payment. This gave them strong incentive (since they would discount the value of future money because of risk) to limit loan terms to six years. That, in turn, put a natural check on the amount most people would borrow, thus making it hard for them to fall into long-term bondage.

Fiat money/currency proclaimed legal tender by the decree of the state, not backed by any precious commodity, is also unbiblical. It violates the Bible's laws against unjust weights and measures[8] by

---

[6] Prov. 22:7
[7] Deut. 15:1-3
[8] Lev. 19:35; Deut. 25:13-16; Prov. 20:10; Isa. 1:21, 22, 24-26

debasing money (inflation). It also is blasphemous, because the state acts as if by its mere decree it can create wealth, something only God can do, as we have already noted.

Working your own way through what the scriptures say about debt, six-year loans, interest on loans, etc., and coming to your own conclusions is a wonderful exercise. I highly recommend it to you. The point I want to make is this: If I really need this thing *now*, and I am willing to go into debt for it, where is Jehovah-Jireh, the "God who provides?" It isn't easy to dig out of debt, if I am already in it. Yet, over the years in watching many, many believers recognize their need for being debt free, I have seen God marvelously meet their needs once they have committed themselves.

## Leveraging through Sacrifice and Hard Work

It is obviously better to pay the price ourselves for what we believe we need, in terms of making personal sacrifice, than to find fault with God and meet the needs our *own way* independent of Him. This is precisely what Satan used to tempt Jesus in the wilderness. Jesus was famished and hungry to the bone after His forty day fast. His options were these: (1) provide for Himself by obeying Satan's suggestion that He "turn stones into bread,"[9] or (2) believe that God would provide—which Jesus did, and God sent angels who fed Him.[10] Jesus said in John 5:30 that, "I can do nothing on my own initiative." What a wonderful example our Master gives us of the truth: God pays for what He orders.

Does this mean that we are to lay around and "wait for God" to bring us the things we need to survive and prosper? Jesus didn't live like that, so why should we? He lived an incredibly active life and told us through the Apostle Paul that, "If anyone will not work, neither let him eat."[11] Remember, God provides both supernaturally and through the sweat of our own brow. This simple but epic Bible verse reminds

---

[9] Matt. 4:3-4
[10] Matt. 4:11
[11] 2 Thess. 3:10

us of this fact. We see God shifting from one mode to the other in His dealings with Israel when He tells them that He will supply their needs, but they must also work.

> And the manna ceased on the day after they
> had eaten some of the produce of the land,
> so that the sons of Israel no longer had
> manna, but they ate some of the yield of the
> land of Canaan during that year.  *Joshua 5:12*

So how do we leverage through sacrifice? Let me give you two classic contemporary examples. Firstly, many (if not most) of the Korean, Chinese, and Vietnamese immigrants to the United States immediately move in with extended family members until they can afford to secure their own housing. It may take ten years, but they would rather save the money first, "leveraging" through personal inconvenience. This allows them to avoid paying two to three times the price of the house through a long-term mortgage. Does this kind of leveraging work? You bet. I have had personal friends who became lawyers, doctors, and dentists as their Asian family and friends cooperatively paid for their education with non-interest loans, rather than give their money to the banks.

The second example is similar and deals with keeping currency circulating through your own particular associates or community. I have seen different studies over the years that monitored the number of times that a dollar bill would go through a particular community before it passed on to those outside of it. The African-American community dollar usually changes hands three to four times within their community; the whites and Latins six to seven times; and the Asians somewhere around twelve. You don't have to be a genius to see what that means:  Keeping resources within a tighter circle makes that circle stronger. Distribution systems that circulate resources internally grow very rapidly. This is the future for wise investors.

We can leverage the future through debt, or we can leverage our way *into* the future through creativity, community commitments, and hard work. God's way is obvious. He pays for what He orders, and He has already ordered, as we have seen, good stewardship, creativity, labor, and cooperation in the brotherhood.

If we want to tie into God's intentions regarding both wealth and riches, not only personally but also corporately, we need to remember that God wants to empower people with His goals and skills, and He wants us to use our wealth to promote this. That's the difference between profit-seeking and servanthood. The difference between Kingdom economics and either socialism or capitalism is this: While socialism's supreme goal is to eliminate risk by making everyone dependent on the state, and capitalism's supreme goal is to make a profit, Kingdom economics focuses on empowering people to be what God created them to be. Using our resources is what makes this happen. When we use our money, time, or skills to reach into someone's life, we can help him fulfill his destiny. Do you want God's blessing? Let Him show you that He pays for what He orders, mostly by creatively leveraging some resource in you or those around you through hard work.

# CHAPTER SEVEN

# Risk, Self-Respect, and Redemptive Struggle

*"Do not be deceived, God is not mocked; for whatever a man sows, this he will also reap."*
Gal. 6:7

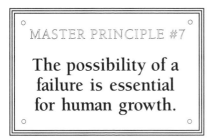

MASTER PRINCIPLE #7

**The possibility of a failure is essential for human growth.**

*A* truly free society encourages obedience to God, is compassionate to the truly needy, and permits man to be freely blessed or penalized as a consequence of his own choices. The opposite is true for the modern liberal state: Its economic policies enslave the needy with ineffective, addictive aid, and it shields large numbers of its citizens from the consequences of their sins with financial policies that promote rebellion against God's laws. Committed to parentalism, the modern state promotes moral failure and penalizes virtue. These are tall charges. Are they really true?

As we touch the issues surrounding the relationship between risk, failure, and moral growth, we will be dealing with the concepts which underpin a society's economic policies in the areas of welfare, insurance and health care policies, and criminal justice. Even after all these years it is still amazing to me how our collective spiritual values (or lack thereof) have such a direct bearing on economic policy. The study of economics is the study of how spiritual choices play themselves out in the material world. As the Almighty's project associates, we must become experts in understanding these basic spiritual/economic relationships. Unless we do, we will be poor citizens and likewise unable to fulfill the Master's great commission of discipling nations with public policy that is built upon observing all that Christ commanded.[1]

---

[1] Matt. 28:18-20

## Self-Respect Comes from God's Feedback System

One of the crises of the modern world is the quest for "authenticity," "meaning," and "self-respect." But all of these necessary and elusive traits only have ultimate meaning if they are given to us by a source greater than our own self. Indeed, honest men and women recognize, as the mountain of self-help and self-acceptance books pile up in both Christian and secular bookstores, that "me liking me" is an exercise in Zen Buddhism: "How can hand grasp hand" or self approve of self? Put another way, which "me" is qualified to authenticate "me"? And how can I accept the validity of the evidence both received and evaluated by my own self? The scripture, as always, says it best: "The heart is more deceitful than all else and is desperately sick; who can understand it?"[2] Amen.

The human heart is elusive, evasive, self-centered, and desperately needs an objective yardstick *outside of itself* to measure where it is. God's answer to the "yardstick" need is the reality of *cause and effect* as revealed in God's Law/Word. Do *this*, and *this* will happen. Plant corn; you'll never get spinach. Unbiblically create debt; you'll lose your freedom. Commit adultery; your self-esteem is destroyed. Jump off a high building; you'll die. Culturally fail to discipline the children; your nation's taxes required to operate your courts and the criminal justice system will skyrocket. Touch the hot stove; you'll burn your hand. Reality is our feedback system. But you can only correctly interpret reality in life the way God has instructed us, and that is through His Word. Without the Word of God as your teaching guide, interpreting reality's feedback system becomes subjective, chaotic, and unreliable and leads us into both confusion and deception.

So why would anyone want to conceal the proper evaluation of the feedback system? Because they don't want to obey the rules, or have others obey the rules. It makes their rebellion harder to hide. So how do those who oppose God's feedback system try to keep men from reading it correctly? Here are two simple techniques: (1) by rejecting and ridiculing the Word of God, and shielding the citizens

---

[2] Jer. 17:9

of a culture from it as much as their society's constitutional law permits; and (2) by using tax dollars to "muffle" the effects of sin on the disobedient by providing them goods and services to lessen the blows of cause-and-effect. Welcome to the truly anti-Christ philosophy behind the liberal modern state. Once you see this truth, it's a mind-boggler.

## The State Resists God's Feedback System

If you fornicate, the state will either directly or indirectly help you kill the child through abortion, or help you raise it using other people's money. If you become addicted to anything, it will help keep you addicted, or pay for help for you, as long as it is not Christian in nature. If you steal, instead of pressing you to make biblical restitution, the state will cage you up at a cost of $25,000 a year at the taxpayer's expense. Commit a "white-collar" crime, and the state will make your stay even nicer. The state will pay subsidies of all kinds to rich and poor alike and rig the game as best it can so that the laws of cause-and-effect are blunted, dulled, and made less obvious. If you somehow awakened to reality and repented, that would look bad for the rest of us. The price tag to all of us is higher taxes, bureaucracy, colossal injustice, and most of all, the trapping of people in their sin.

The state keeps people enslaved because they have the tax resources to do so. What is worse is that the modern state adds insult to injury and does so in the name of "compassion"! This false earthly compassion is economic futility and immoral co-dependency of the worst order, followed by eternal Hell for its victims! That, friend, is some kind of "compassion." God's Word perfectly pierces the smoke-and-mirrors of the modern welfare taxation policy which does this, summing up the matter with the following truth: "The compassion of the wicked is cruel."[3]

---

[3] Prov. 12:10

We'll talk more about the public policy implications of this later, but what does all this have to do with the nature of self-respect? A great, great deal. Self-respect is built on the fact that God and His feedback system are set up to reveal whether or not you're pleasing Him and moving in the right direction. The false protection and false compassion we are exposing here will not let the "ball of life" bounce back to you in truth. It either doesn't come back to you at all, or comes back at lying angles. That's what false compassion does: It lies, and therefore destroys any possibility of true self-respect.

Scripture says that "the fear of the Lord is the beginning of knowledge."[4] In the game of life, I recognize that both God and His universe can play rough and hard. This is the first ultimate reality I must accept and build my life around. We serve a God who doesn't rig the game and who has enough moral courage to let people go to Hell. Why? Is it because He's a mean-spirited, vindictive God as some have foolishly reasoned? No. It's because God recognizes that without the possibility of failure, success would have no meaning. Our God is very deep, to say the least.

If I can't fail, I can't truly succeed. And if I do succeed without the possibility of failure, where is my self-respect? The game was actually rigged; the yardstick of reality was in fact made of elastic compromise! The liberal denies men self-respect by demanding that the state supply a safety net under the universe's trapeze and high wire act.

## Rewards and Penalties Teach Us Reality

Rewards and penalties teach us God's limits and God's way. He leads us by the rod[5] of adversity, as sin is revealed and character forged. By the staff[6] of His protection and provision we stay within the pasture of obedience to His Word and guidance. The reality and risk of penalty teach us dependency and obedience to Christ and the

---

[4] Prov. 1:7
[5] Psa. 23:4
[6] Psa. 23:4

necessity for the power of the Holy Spirit within us to enable us to obey Him. Those who shield us from failure ultimately produce our dependence upon them rather than God. That is slavery to sin and unreality. No self-respect can be found behind a false shield, and those who offer me a false shield are really acting as my enemy, all in the name of "caring."

Even the mottos on the walls of our gyms and exercise rooms preach a truer gospel than the liberals. They say, "No pain, no gain." And so God has made it. The possibility of failure and pain is essential for human growth. Rig the game through false compassion, and you trap your dependent victims in their sins. Welcome to an economy drowning in a sea of red ink called "false help."

### Exposing the Modern State As a False Parent

*When the earth experiences Thy judgments, the inhabitants of the world learn righteousness.*                                                Isa. 26:9

In the name of compassion, the modern state is committed to minimizing the risks of life for all its citizens. It is at war with God's laws of sowing and reaping. It is committed to shield the disobedient from correction, and the successful from "too much success." It also shields those who lawfully play the loopholes of the law to keep from getting caught, especially if they are a part of the power structure. It is a false parent, protecting its citizens from a "mean" God. "The state will save," it says, "not God." And it does so through taxation.

While it is beyond the scope of an introductory book on biblical economics to discuss the "state as savior," I must make one specific application here. As immoral as abortion is, it will not be the ultimate justification for God's judgment against the modern state. This is also true of legalized pornography, unbiblical discrimination, exploitation, and the long litany of our current social ills. God will ultimately judge us economically for *keeping the people from turning to God and using tax money to do it.* This is an *eternal injustice* towards mankind, and an act of self-exalting opposition to God by the state. Economic judgment is inevitable, and its root goes deeper than our absurd and immoral monetary and fiscal policies. It is because our economic policy opposes the very *salvation* of God Himself. The modern state has become a false and treacherous economic shield against God's cause-and-effect correction devices. False love leads to death and to hell.

## If You Really Love Me, Let Me Struggle

If you really love me, you won't get in the way of my struggles with self, sin, growth, and God. Remember, life was tough even for Jesus: "Although He was a Son, He learned obedience from the things which He suffered."[7] Let me give two illustrations that serve our point.

The first is a strong illustration from nature and tells of a little boy who sees a moth fighting its way out of its cocoon. Stopping to help it, out of compassion, he pulls out his trusty pocketknife and carefully slits open the cocoon. The moth comes out, but it dies. Why? There is something the little boy doesn't know: The moth gains the strength necessary to survive as it resists the constrictiveness of the cocoon in its battle to get out. Cut the cocoon, and it dies. How many dead and crippled human beings are on the bloodstained hands of a civil government who cut those people's cocoons and contributed to the destruction of their souls?

The second illustration asks you to make a choice based on the same principle. Suppose our nation is at war, and you get drafted. We're an "emancipated" nation, ladies, so you also get to go to the front and fight next to the men. You're off to boot camp to get combat ready. But this is a modern army of choice: You can go to Drill Sergeant Jones (who has a reputation for being a tough, cruel disciplinarian and makes boot camp a living hell), or you can go to Drill Sergeant Smith (who is a genuinely concerned, compassionate, and sensitive trainer). Which drill sergeant do you choose?

I know which one I want: Drill Sergeant Jones. Give me a mean, dirty, tough instructor whom I may curse in boot camp, but bless on the battlefield because he trained me to stay alive! The kinder, gentler

---

[7] Heb. 5:8

Mr. Smith is no friend of mine even though I may like him as a person far better. Sergeant Jones obviously knows the real issue: Like him or hate him, he couldn't give a rip. His job is to keep you alive. Ultimately, that's real love. That's why God plays "hard ball," and His laws are sometimes tough. Those laws are designed to keep us from eternal death.

As an employer or a civil leader, you must understand that sparing people the consequences of disobedience destroys them, because failure and God's chastisement teach people the fear of the Lord. If you shield people from consequences, you are shielding them from the fear of the Lord, and you're destroying their possibility for true, earned self-respect. That respect comes from doing it right, asking no favors, and cutting yourself no slack.

Our generation grew up under parents who were instructed in secular child rearing, not by the Bible. "Don't you dare spank little Johnny!" they told us. "The Bible is an archaic book. You've got to be a child abuser if you bruise poor little Johnny's ego or bottom. If you do that, he'll grow up to be a social cripple!" A generation that went through the Great Depression and vowed never to let their children go hungry bought that nonsense. The result? The next generation seldom learned responsibility because it seldom faced consequences.

Everybody looked at the young people of the sixties and asked, "How could this be?" They should have asked, "How could this not be?" The sixties generation wasn't taught about the cost of sin. Now we are paying the bill.

Godly relationships, not civil government, should sustain us when we have needs; primarily, that means the family and not some kind of "mother state."

The state as an indulgent, sheltering mother is destroying the family. Who stepped in to shield a man and woman from dealing properly with sin and its consequences in marriage? It was the state who said, "You don't need to work it out in covenant. Get a divorce. And if you get into financial trouble, we'll cushion you. You won't go hungry. You won't go without a roof. We're the ultimate safety net."

When the state says, "We will support you, whatever happens," it destroys the family and turns people into slaves.

What is the cause of homelessness? It's the destruction of the family. What will solve homelessness? It won't be building shelters for the homeless; that will only expand the problem. Instead, we should give the homeless a one-way ticket to their nearest kin. Believe it or not, I really mean that. Send the homeless home if they have one. Give them a one-way ticket and a letter saying, "It is our joy to help reunite you with your nearest living kin. You will not get another of these tickets. Neither will you get any more welfare." Add a letter to their kin saying, "Your sister is on the way to your house. You're a family. Make it work. Signed, The State." This may sound "tough" and void of compassion, but think about the long run alternative consequences. Don't make the homeless more dependent on government handouts. Show real compassion, the kind that cares more about their growth in character and their eternal destiny than their immediate convenience.

### What's True Love: Truth or Lies?

Some people will object. "You don't understand. I don't like my mother. I don't like my father. I don't like my brothers, my sisters, my relatives. And they don't like me!"

The proper response? "Why should everyone else pay for your family's hassles? The government shouldn't reach into everyone's wallet to pay the price for your bickering with your sister. Go home! By God's grace, work it out. And if you won't, don't foist your problems off on somebody else."

Our economic policy has to have a slogan beneath it: "Go home." Go home for care, for housing, for wealth creation. Go home to lay up treasure for your children. Don't go to the state. Go home!

And by the way, this isn't coming from a heartless Christian fascist. In our own city, our church leader's group has helped to house, feed, and clothe most of our city's homeless all winter for the last several years, without a pile of the federal or state government's help, I might add. But we know that we're only a stopgap measure, and we do encourage them to either go home or become responsible enough to create their own home.

Of course, the modern state doesn't want to hear this kind of truth. After all, it has its science, technology, the media, and its monetary and fiscal policy to help it continue to play the false, shielding parent to its citizens. And it has the printing presses to run out more money and the ability to create new money in the banking systems' balance sheets. The state can circumvent the consequences of inferior work, government waste, a lack of planning, and resource confiscation through unbiblical taxation. It seems "responsible" to minimize life's risks. So what? Here's what.

Today we are rapidly approaching the time when God will say, "Okay, I gave you acid indigestion, but you didn't respond. So go ahead and print your money. I will take My hands off, and your indigestion will become a cancerous stomach that will certainly immobilize you."

One of the most terrifying passages in all of God's Word is, "Ephraim is joined to idols; let him alone."[8] As long as God deals with you, you have hope. When He stops, you are in trouble. If you continue to rebel, God says, "All right, I will take My hands off of you and let your disobedience bring forth its own judgment."

That's what has happened to the United States. Instead of looking at the causes of our troubles, we have succumbed to the idolatrous notion that civil government can create money (which it mistakes for real riches and even for wealth) out of nothing, and that we can use this created money to buy our way out of the consequences of sin. God says, "All right, you think you can print enough money to escape judgment? Let's see how fast your presses can run. They can't outrun My judgment..."

---

[8] Hosea 4:17

### Recognizing Eight Cocoon-Cutting Economic Policies
### Destroying Our Nation

Do you enjoy sending more than forty-five percent of everything you earn, in the form of direct and indirect taxes, to the government to continue this cruel joke? Let's listen carefully to this "jokester's" reasoning so we can vote him out of office when we hear him speaking these lies:

1. "Authority must be increasingly centralized in the state. After all, no one has the resources to solve problems like the state."

2. "Case law and bureaucratic law must gently replace constitutional law if the people who really need help and protection are to get it. The original founders of the Constitution lived in an agrarian-based culture and foresaw few of the pluralistic, urban-based problems of a democracy today. Their wisdom is dated and outmoded."

3. "In order to provide a just and compassionate safety net, taxes must be raised to provide adequate services. Those who have prospered by greed, social status, and sheer luck should obviously share their wealth with victims of life's accidents and society's prejudices."

4. "Private property is a far lesser right than compassion. Cough more of it up."

5. "Your children belong to the state in terms of their educational needs. Parents are usually well-meaning but incompetent, and their personal prejudices and preferences may prove harmful to the children in terms of preparing them to live in peace with all people, values, and life-styles in the context of modern democracy."

6. "Production and trade must be carefully regulated by the state. If we do not protect our jobs and citizens in the economics of the global market, who will?"

7. "The state will guarantee the ultimate litmus test of a society's true freedom: consenting adult sexual freedom. If the state stays out of your bedroom, even if it's in your board room, you are truly free."

8. "What is good for this generation should be the best test of policy and lifestyle decision making. Each generation must be free to choose how it would live, unencumbered by the prejudices of the past and the pressures of attempting to define and resolve the elusive challenges of future generations' problems."

Behind each of these cocoon-cutting statements lurks a mountain of our current economic-death policies and unreality, but I spare you.

## Jesus Takes Poverty Out of People, Not People Out of Poverty

While chapter eight will focus more precisely on the relationship between poverty and sin, we must mention this relationship in the context of "risk" and its relationship to poverty. Minimizing people's risk, or attempting to do so, frequently leads them into irresponsibility which ultimately leads to poverty. God's answer to poverty is responsibility for choices, actions, and consequences. To limit any of these three leads to a loss of freedom, and a loss of freedom automatically leads to poverty, since poverty is perhaps best defined as having fewer and fewer productive choices.

Poverty is a *spiritual disease* more than an economic condition. Put more precisely, it is an inner disease of soul and spirit that manifests itself in the natural outer world by a scarcity of resources. Poverty is a set of choices which become a lifestyle. Its spiritual causes are clearly identified throughout the book of Proverbs. They include several things: laziness, fear, get-rich-quick schemes, disobedience, anger, dishonesty, bribery, idolatry, adultery, and theft. To become free of external scarcity, I must first remove it internally from myself. Both poverty and prosperity begin on the inside of us.

The state cannot cure a spiritual disease with money. That is another cocoon-cutting tactic. While compassion is essential, and supplying the opportunity to glean for oneself is an attribute of a free society,[9] unearned money is not the answer. It is a pocketknife in another form, designed to cut a cocoon. Unless the money is issued in the form of a repayable, non-interest bearing loan,[10] it is principally unjust to both the self-respect of the recipient and the freedom of the taxpayer from whom the revenue was secured. If that sounds tough, don't blame me. Blame our "mean" God. After all, what does the One who hung on the Cross know about real compassion? My sarcasm has a point: Truth is ultimate compassion.

## Poverty Is about Skills, Not Money

Charles Murray's book, *Losing Ground,*[11] an economic study of the so-called "War on Poverty" Programs, is familiar to most serious students of state planned cocoon-cutting in the United States. The study demonstrated (and to my knowledge remains unrefuted) the total futility of giving direct financial aid to the poor without stipulations for repayment. In the end, the recipients of these substantial amounts of dollars in the slum-laden Chicago neighborhoods came out poorer, not richer. No internal wealth was created in the people who received the money; what else could we expect but more external poverty?

God delivers us from poverty in Christ. His Word promised those who obeyed the laws of His redeemed community, "but you shall remember the Lord your God, for it is He who is giving you power to make wealth, that He may confirm His Covenant which He swore to your fathers, as it is this day."[12]

But how can I experience the way to that promise if you don't let me live out the consequences of my failures? Failures instruct me *on* the way and *in* the way. Without the possibility of living in my failures, I'll never grow up. ALMIGHTY & SONS is built on risk

---

[9] Lev. 19:9-10
[10] Ex. 22:25; Deut. 23:19-20; Neh. 5:11-13
[11] Losing *Ground: American Social Policy in the 1950-80's,* New York, Basis Books 1984
[12] Deut. 8:18

taking. That is what makes Heaven incredibly meaningful. We really could have gone the other way: The game isn't rigged. Because it isn't rigged, I rejoice in God's saving mercy to me, and I can hold my head up because once I caught the ball, I ran with it. That is far better than "self-esteem." That is called "self-respect."

# CHAPTER EIGHT

# Exposing the Cruelty
# of the Economics of Blame

*"Let him who steals steal no longer; but rather let him labor, performing with his own hands what is good, in order that he may have something to share with him who has need."*                                    Eph. 4:28

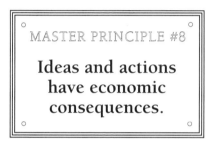

MASTER PRINCIPLE #8

**Ideas and actions
have economic
consequences.**

The world system wants us to believe that poverty and injustice are things that "happen" to people, like having an accident or falling in love. You have no control over poverty; rather it is something that is caused by others (exploitation), fate (chance), or a very strange God. Christians ought to know better for, biblically speaking, poverty is always associated with the curses of man's fallenness. But what the modern world has given to us is the economic reasoning of blame and hate. They're not only ugly, but also they don't work.

It is not necessarily a virtue to be rich; indeed we are repeatedly warned against its dangers and potential idolatries.[1] But poverty, on the other hand, is absolutely no sign of God's blessing. Hopefully, our preceding chapters have convinced you or reinforced this truth for you. So where does poverty come from? And why is the world system so intent on getting you and me to feel guilty for any material blessings we have, on the one hand, while seeking to get us to purchase more than we can afford on the other? Why are they also trying to get us to feel sorry for those who are poor, who mysteriously got hit by the "poverty truck?" Their poverty is obviously somebody's fault other than their own. Or is it?

---

[1] Prov. 28; 23:5; Eccl. 4.8; Matt. 13:22; 1 Tim. 6:9

## Poverty Is the Fruit of Sin

The Bible says that ideas and actions have consequences. That is why the whole theme of the scriptures focuses on right thinking, doctrine, truth, sin, repentance, and aligning our thoughts, faith, and actions with Christ's. As the scripture puts it, "As a man thinketh in his heart, so is he."[2] Indeed, our thinking patterns lead to actions, and actions form habits and character, which lead to the consequences of the law of sowing and reaping. It's clear that sowing and reaping produces economic consequences in terms of our stewardship skills, work habits, savings and consumption patterns, honesty, ability to cooperate, service orientation, and the like. All these characteristics, and others, directly affect the financial strengths of individuals, businesses, and even nations, especially in terms of foreign and domestic economic aid and development. Why nations should fund other nations' sins remains a mystery to me.

Ideas and actions do have economic consequences, and poverty can be one of them. While called to be compassionate to the poor, and always mindful of sharing with them, believers likewise are called to understand poverty and avoid its clutches.[3]

Poverty is the result of sin: be it personal sin, parental sin, social sin, or national sin. Because it is "sin based," poverty won't just go away by throwing money at it as we have already seen. Neither will it go away by spreading blame.

The writer of Hebrews tells us that the things that were visible are shadows, or types of eternal things which we don't see.[4] Spiritual law undergirds and governs the material creation. Unfortunately, we tend to forget this principle when it comes to economics. Rather than recognizing the spiritual laws that undergird moral consequences, cause-and-effect relationships, and the unfailing connections between obedience and blessing (on the one hand) and disobedience and cursing (on the other hand), we tend to see wealth as "luck" and poverty as "victimization." Secular humanism then insists that civil government,

---

[2] Prov. 23:7 KJV
[3] Eph. 4:28
[4] Heb. 9:23-24

which God ordained to enforce justice, must equalize wealth by redistributing it from the lucky to the victimized. What we learn, if we take scripture seriously, is that although some poverty does stem from oppression, most poverty is the consequence of spiritual disobedience, and God calls civil government to enforce obedience to His Law, not to avert His discipline on those who disobey Him.

## Chance or Design?

The difference between these views is the difference between a chance-dominated and a design-dominated understanding of all of reality. One view tells us that wealth and poverty happen to people purely by chance, and that only civil government's interference can alleviate poverty. The other tells us that wealth and poverty are rooted in people's living according to, or contrary to, the design God wove into creation. With the latter view, we see that the real purpose of civil government is not to prevent the consequences of disobedience, but to uphold the order of creation so that people can learn (from moral and material cause-and-effect relationships) to be responsible and obedient to God. We have seen this truth in previous chapters, especially chapter seven.

The laws of nature are in fact ordered responses to the moral government God built into His creation. If you jump off a bridge, the law of gravity doesn't victimize you; you victimize yourself by violating God's Law. The law of entropy, which Paul in Romans 8 called the law of "sin and death," says that matter and energy tend naturally toward dissolution. Sin brought entropy into creation. We're not victimized by the law; we contribute to it in our sin. When we live as if the law of entropy weren't true (failing to work hard, save, and invest), then the law of entropy will ensure that we become poor.[5]

The business world is built on the laws of supply and demand. As the supply of goods or a service increases relative to the demand for it, its price must fall, and vice versa.[6] When the state tries to act as if the

---

[5]Prov. 6:6-11; 24:30-34
[6]1 Kings 10:21, 27; 2 Kings 6:25; 7:1, 16; Prov. 27:7

laws of supply and demand were myths, it creates new money out of nothing. Then the inflated money supply drives prices through the roof. The people aren't victimized by the laws of supply and demand; they're victimized by the rebellious, God-rejecting state.

The law of service and exaltation (whoever serves will be exalted), is a law God has put into His universe.[7] Just as promotion doesn't happen by chance to good servants,[8] so demotion doesn't happen by chance to wicked servants.[9] This does not mean that children, born to parents whose spiritual disobedience has made them poor, aren't victims. They are. Many generations of poor people have been born into the consequences of slavery and family disintegration. In that sense, they really are victims.

### A Call for Economic Discipleship

True, many have been victimized for generations by being deprived of capital accumulation. But giving them money won't deliver them from poverty. Why? Because, as we saw in chapter two, the stewardship skills of properly utilizing private property are essential to maturity. Because many poor people have been kept from accumulating capital, they have had no practice in stewarding private property. Hence, they have remained dependent and irresponsible. Putting money into their hands only makes it easy for them to be bad stewards of it. Instead, like anyone who was never trained in excellent stewardship, they need to be taught, usually one-on-one, to be mature stewards. This is primarily the Christians' job, and we have failed miserably at it. The poor need to be led in obedience to God's Law. Then they will develop wealth, character, and skills that will enable them to produce riches.

This is nothing new. It's the same underlying principle that makes true the old saying attributed to Native Americans, "Give a man a fish, and you feed him for a day. Teach him to fish, and you feed him

---

[7]Phil. 2:8-9; 1 Peter 5:1-7
[8]Prov. 14:35; 17:2; 22:29; Matt. 24:45-47; 25:20-23; Luke 19:16-19, 26
[9]Matt. 25:24-28, 30; Luke 19:20-25, 27; 20:9-18

for a lifetime." The real biblical answer is one-on-one discipleship. It ought to be going on in every city, led by the Christian business community in concert with the local churches. Any business system that trains and disciples people economically will be blessed of God. Count on it.

### God's Word Tells Us How to Avoid the Snares of Poverty

There are *many* scriptures dealing with the causes of poverty. Let's let God's Word speak for itself and see what it says through some of these:

> **Prov. 11:24**—There is one who scatters, yet increases all the more, and there is one who withholds what is justly due, but it results only in want. **(Dishonesty)**

> **Prov. 13:18**—Poverty and shame will come to him who neglects discipline, but he who regards reproof will be honored. **(Laziness)**

> **Prov. 13:21**—Adversity pursues sinners, but the righteous will be rewarded with prosperity. **(Sin)**

> **Prov. 14:23**—In all labor there is profit, but mere talk leads only to poverty. **(Laziness)**

> **Prov. 19:15**—Laziness casts into a deep sleep, and an idle man will suffer hunger. **(Laziness)**

> **Prov. 23:20-21**—Do not be with heavy drinkers of wine, or with gluttonous eaters of meat; for the heavy drinker and the glutton will come to poverty, and drowsiness will clothe a man with rags. **(Poor stewardship)**

> **Prov. 28:19**—He who tills his land will have plenty of food, but he who follows empty pursuits will have poverty in plenty. **(Laziness)**

> **Prov. 28:20**—A faithful man will abound with blessings, but he who makes haste to be rich will not go unpunished. **(Get rich quick mentality)**

> **Prov. 28:22**—A man with an evil eye hastens after wealth, and does not know that want will come upon him. **(Greed)**
>
> **Prov. 30:8**—Keep deception and lies far from me, give me neither poverty nor riches; feed me with the food that is my portion. **(Discontentment)**
>
> **Jer. 17:11**—As a partridge that hatches eggs which it has not laid, so is he who makes a fortune, but unjustly; in the midst of his days it will forsake him, and in the end he will be a fool. **(Dishonesty)**

This does give us a clear picture of at least one thing: Poverty is a result of some attitude or action. It doesn't just happen. If you want to escape it, you must trade ideas for ideas, old ideas for new vision, and thus replace old actions with new actions (i.e., repentance).

### Man Wants to Blame His Environment for Poverty

The first visible evidence of man's fallenness in the Garden was his attempt to solve the problem of his own nakedness by his own devices.[10] The second was his attempt to hide his new-found disobedient knowledge from his Creator.[11] The third was to blame God's environment as the excuse for his fallen condition.[12] Nothing has changed, and fallen man still approaches his problems using all three of these excuses. They may be more "complex and scientific," but they still amount to the same old methods.

The three greatest examples of twentieth century man blaming his faulty environment for poverty, in particular, are psychological determinism (Freudianism), economic determinism (Marxism), and biological determinism (Darwinism). These deadly "blame triplets" have cost the wealth producers multi-billions of confiscated tax dollars, which were cruelly wasted. They have inflamed men to hatred and wars, and generally wrought havoc on the last century. These three

---

[10]Gen. 3:7
[11]Gen. 3:8
[12]Gen. 3:12-13

ideas haven't solved poverty, either. Let's take a quick glance at each one of the three.

## The Trap of Psychological Blame

First, psychological determinism essentially claims that sin and poverty are caused by our personal inability to resolve internal conflicts with our parents and the values they superimposed upon us. Freud and his disciples point out that man is primarily, or exclusively, a soul and body entity with no spirit. Therefore, how people treat us determines what we become. We are all "victims" since all of us have been mistreated. Poverty from this vantage is just the economic symptom of unresolved internal psychological and external relational trauma. My Ego, Id, and Super-ego did the dirty deed, and all I have to show for it is the scattered debris of my unresolved libidinal energies polluting myself and others like nuclear fallout.

## The Trap of Class Warfare and Environmental Blame

Secondly, economic determinism tells us that all human relationships are determined by the ownership and distribution of private property, and the means of production (what you have and how you get it). Class warfare results from the systematic rationalization that the "have's" are oppressing the "have not's." It suggests that personal poverty is forced upon you by the period in history, society, and station of life in which you chanced to be born. Marx and his ideological children have destroyed countless millions of humans with his fabric of rationalizations in the nineteenth and twentieth centuries. Their blame/hating system created a class consciousness with its attendant guilt and envy that only time and Jesus can cleanse from us.

## The Trap of Biological Blame

Third, Darwin and his biological determinism want us to believe that it is the amount of strength in our heredity which determines our station in life. Genetic codes and parental genes compel us to become whatever we become. We are victims of chance procreation, not asking to be born, but stuck with the biological cards we've been dealt from our parents and race. The fittest survive and dominate, while the victims of the weaker genes are dominated and poverty-laden.

There may be kernels of misapplied truths in all three systems, and we must recognize that. Humanly speaking, though our parental environment plays a significant role in the formation of who we are, it is not all determining. God holds all of us responsible for how we *play* the cards He dealt us. Indeed, correctly reading those cards is the key to interpreting our destiny and purpose in life and beginning to fulfill it. God pays for what He orders, and my strengths and weaknesses, on every level, were permitted for a purpose and a reason. Our job is to find that purpose in and through Christ and to use our internal and external circumstances to grow in grace and serve God and others. What I was given was my destiny. What "victimizes" me is the way I make excuses for how I respond. I cannot control all that happens to me, but I am commanded to control my responses.[13] Many poor kids grew up and worked their way to success, and many "golden spoon" kids grew up to be failures. Environment isn't the issue: obedience to spiritual law is.

### Let's Trash Blame and Expose the Real Root Causes of Poverty

*"...the axe is already laid at the root of the trees..."* Matt. 3:10

In one sense, seeking the causes of poverty can be a fruitless exercise. Since the fall of man, poverty has been the natural condition of mankind. It certainly has been the general condition of mankind throughout history. That is why Adam Smith titled his great book, *An Inquiry into the Nature and Cause of the Wealth of Nations.* He realized that the truly interesting question was not what makes some people

---

[13]Gen. 4:7

and nations poor (all would naturally be poor), but what makes some wealthy. That, in a fallen world, is the smart question.

## Five Enemies to Be Destroyed

1) **Fear.** It is no accident that modern science is based upon a belief in laws that in fact were created by God. The pagan view of reality sees no link between cause and effect because it recognizes no systematic laws in a universe governed by a systematic God. Belief in an ordered, covenantal universe is an exclusively Christian concept. All pagan religions and philosophies believe in capricious gods who continually change the rules according to their own personality flaws. But science is built on predictability. Christians believe in predictability because they believe God has covenantally put in motion laws of cause-and-effect.

Many Christians talk about faith as if it were some kind of mystical concept. But the promise of faith is the simple idea that God created the universe and holds it in predictability because of His covenant with creation. If we do a certain thing, we can be sure that God will respond in a certain way. That is faith: the conviction that you live under the covenant of your Creator. And faith is the opposite of fear.

People who don't believe they live under the covenant of their Creator will not invest in the future, because it will be too unpredictable. Instead, they will live in constant fear of the future. That is why capitalism flourishes only where a biblical worldview flourishes. Capitalism is based on investing current resources into the future based on the faithfulness (predictability) of a covenant-keeping God who promises that if you invest, work hard, and obey Him, He will reward your investment. Disobedient fear is an assault against God's character. That is why it can't produce anything but failure.

This is why the principles we are teaching are so important. America's growing rejection of biblical Christianity is bearing fruit in reduced investment in the future because paganism lacks faith in a covenant-keeping God. Why invest if you have no assurance that God, in faithfulness to His covenant, will reward you? The more pagan a culture becomes, the less it will invest in the future. The Bible says that the just shall live by faith.[14] Economically, this means that the just will believe that if they invest according to God's will and obey Him, His predictable universe will yield a predictable result of increase.

**2) Greed.** It is a common notion that the rich are greedy and the poor are not. The truth is that a man's circumstances do not determine the attitude of his heart. The attitude of his heart, however, may well determine his circumstances. And if his heart is greedy, it is more likely that he will become poor, not rich.

Why? Stated simply, it is because greed is a form of discontent, an unwillingness to live contentedly in one's circumstances. Greed demands the enjoyment of more wealth than one presently has, and it demands it *now*. If someone can't produce more wealth by investing his own time, energy, and money into productive enterprise, greed will drive him to try to increase his wealth by borrowing for consumption, or by theft. Both ways lead, in the long-run, to poverty, either because a thief is put in jail or because a compulsive borrower sees his income consumed by interest payments. If he escapes these twin destroyers he may fall to the third: catastrophic loss due to foolish investing in "getting rich quick" schemes which appeal to his greed.

**3) Laziness.** The connection between laziness and poverty is clear and direct. "Poor is he who works with a negligent hand, But the hand of the diligent makes rich."[15] Indeed, the book of Proverbs is filled with passages tying laziness to poverty as we have seen. The simple fact is that wealth is produced by work; to the extent that people don't work, they don't create wealth. And those who don't create wealth become dependent on the wealth of others for survival. That is why Paul so sternly commanded, "If anyone will not work, neither let him eat."[16]

**4) Idolatry and Paganism.** I work with a group of Mexican Christians in Juarez, Mexico. The leadership there has taken a garbage

---

[14] Hab. 2:4
[15] Prov. 10:4
[16] 2 Thess. 3:10

dump and turned it into a city set on a hill. They've built houses and put in a medical/dental clinic and a school, a home with a hundred children, and businesses that employ numbers of families. It's a flourishing model of what can happen when the concepts in this book are applied.

One evening I was up on the roof there, looking out across the Rio Grande into El Paso. The river marks a massive transition in the quality of life, economically speaking. I prayed, "Lord, explain to me what I see." The minerals on both sides of the river were the same; the climate was the same; and the opportunity to develop the resources was the same. But God showed me that what made all the difference were spiritual concepts. You can see it like night and day in going from Juarez to El Paso. Juarez and El Paso are dominated by different spiritual views of the world, and those differing views have vast consequences.

Humberto Belli, former education minister in the democratically elected Nicaraguan government that replaced the Communist Sandinistas, and the theologian Ronald Nash, point out that most of Latin America's economic woes are rooted in moral and cultural deficiencies. Here is a list: an anti-work ethic connected with the Spanish ideal of the *hidalgo*, the landed gentry who needn't work for a living; amoral familism, the notion that one owes loyalty and truthfulness only to one's family and close relatives and to no one else; pervasive dishonesty and corruption; and a focus on immediate self-gratification rather than long-term investment. At the root of all these, they see the most fundamental problem: a people never truly converted to the Christian faith. To really appreciate ideas in action, go to El Paso-Juarez; it will show you blatant economic reality. Ideas do have consequences.

**5) Single-Generation Consumption.** Have you ever driven along the freeway and seen the bumper sticker, "I'm spending my children's inheritance"? Four-letter words would be less offensive! The Bible says parents ought to store up wealth for their children. A portion of what you accumulate belongs to your children, not to you.

Can you imagine stealing your son's paper route money or your daughter's baby-sitting money? Yet that's exactly what inflation, our fiat money policy, does. That's exactly what one generational consumption does. We sneak into our children's rooms at night and take what doesn't belong to us. That's why the national debt is a spiritual outrage. It is theft from our children.

In short, poverty is rooted in the rejection of Christianity, its view of reality, and its disciplines. Now, how does our society attempt to deal with poverty?

Paganism cannot explain differences in wealth because it doesn't have a concept of the covenant. When it sees inequality, it says, "This must be wrong. Why should these people be wealthy and these people be poor?" It never asks, "What have these people done to accumulate what they've got, and what have these people done who do not have it?"

Our intent is not to justify all the rich regardless of how they got rich. After all, we're after wealth, not riches. But what does the Bible say? To him that has, what will happen? He's going to be given more. Why? Because he has the covenantal skills, character, and blessing that God, the ultimate Investment Banker in the Cosmos, is seeking.

God wants a high return on His investment. Remember, He's the One who collected the crumbs from the loaves and fishes so that nothing would be lost. That shows us Father's nature. He says, "Whoever I can find that I can trust with increase, I'm going to give him more to steward. You've been faithful over two minas, so I'm going to put you over two cities." From those who have misused what they have, He takes away even what remains.

As we begin to inject biblical economics into our culture, we will reward good stewards, instead of penalizing them. Then we will work to transform bad stewards into good stewards by investing in them as disciples and imparting character and skills to them, rather than making them comfortable in their irresponsibility. With biblical economics, we're going to see a huge and swelling increase in the prosperity of the nations and their people.

God wants us to recognize the difference between pure charity, with no strings attached (which Christians should extend voluntarily, but only to those who, through no fault of their own, are truly unable to care for themselves), and investment, which has rewards and penalties. Our message to every poor person who is neither mentally nor physically disabled should be, "If you handle what we've invested in you, you get more, and if you misuse it, we'll take it away and give it to someone who handles it wisely." Is that cruel? No. That's love, because it forces people to deal with the consequences of their own actions, rather than hide behind the prison bars of blame and accusation which make enemies of men. False compassion produces hate, and its ugly tentacles continue to spread its deadly lies within our "wrong-headed" culture.

While the Bible recognizes personal sin, cultural sin, and generational sin[17] as contributors to the obstacles we must overcome through Christ's power, it also recognizes man's penchant for convenience ahead of practical provision. The following scripture is loaded with practical insight and application. I commend it to your meditation. It clearly tells us to look first to our provision and then to our comfort:

> Prepare your work outside,
> And make it ready for yourself in the field;
> Afterwards, then, build your house.
>
> *Prov. 24:27*

## God's Answer to Blame Is a Vision of Change
## and the Discipline to Do It

For several years I helped local communities to form "City Action Councils" where Christians pool their skills and resources to help solve community problems. Some of the results have been outstanding. Numbers of churches and believers throughout the world are beginning

---

[17] Num. 14:18

to get creatively involved in helping share economic wealth with others. With the emergence of increasing economic judgment against our culture, the Church and the entire private sector must play an expanding role in serving and empowering the needy and untrained. What we need to accomplish this are men and women infected with dreams, vision, skill, and discipline, rather than the "gimmies" and the "this is your fault," type of people.

Briefly, I would like to mention the four major methods God sets before us relative to alleviating poverty in others:

1. **Creating opportunities for gleaning** (Lev. 19:9-10):

   The scripture teaches that those in need have an obligation to provide for themselves through their own labor, even if the resources they are using are provided freely. As we've already seen, to pay someone for doing nothing is to make them feel like "nothing." Israel, as an agrarian based culture, supplied food for the needy by not harvesting the whole fields or crops. How can we apply this principle in a modern culture so that supply is free but labor must be self-generated? The principle is clear, and there are some creative answers. How can you make what you produce available to those truly in need in exchange for their labor? Almighty's business partners must learn to operate like their Father: The "living water" is free (grace), but you must supply your own container (life and commitment).

2. **Making non-interest bearing loans available to the brethren:**

   One way to financially empower the needy, at least amongst believers in particular, is to make non-interest bearing loans available to them, like Israel did,[18] for specific periods of time. Interest is the rent charged for using someone else's resources (money). Non-interest bearing loans specifically fulfill the spirit of what Christ taught us in the Sermon on the Mount in terms of non-reciprocal gifts, charity, and love for those in genuine need.

---

[18]Lev. 25:35-37

3. **Voluntary servitude:**

   Scripture's primary "welfare system," as patterned in Israel,[19] was direct discipleship through contractual service. If you were in either poverty or what we would call bankruptcy, you could sell your labor to someone who knew how to disciple you for up to six full years. While the exact laws pertaining to these relationships would likely be unacceptable for most people today, it was *principally* an ingenious system of transferring the *wealth skills* of someone who had their life together to someone who did not, without making them feel like a fool or an incompetent. Instead of welfare checks, they got work assignments, and beyond that, they received a total exposure to the *full lifestyle* of the one discipling them. Some form of this character building approach must be developed if we are to have any realistic hope of freeing people from the course of poverty with their dignity intact. This biblical approach to removing poverty requires personal discipling rather than the indirect approach of government subsidies, social workers, and arms-length help.

4. **A primary focus on displaying Almighty's love in practical ways:**

   Isaiah 58:6-12 is among the most powerful and moving sections of scripture. To read it is to get an instant "gut check" on how much we carry God's heart for the truly needy and to begin to ask ourselves the right questions on what practical steps we can take. I know some Christian leaders who have come up with a number of wonderful practical answers to the question of effective service and evangelism through it.[20] The promises contained in this set of scriptures are awe-inspiring:

   > Is this not the fast which I choose, to loosen
   > the bonds of wickedness, to undo the bands

---

[19] Lev. 25:39-55

[20] *Conspiracy of Kindness*—Steve Shogren. I heartily recommend this book on practical ways to evangelize through serving others and seeing their needs as an opportunity of sharing life.

of the yoke, and to let the oppressed go free,
and break every yoke? Is it not to divide
your bread with the hungry, and bring the
homeless poor into the house; when you see
the naked, to cover him; and not to hide
yourself from your own flesh? Then your
light will break out like the dawn, and your
recovery will speedily spring forth; and your
righteousness will go before you; the glory of
the Lord will be your rear guard. Then you
will call, and the Lord will answer; you will
cry, and He will say, "Here I am." If you
remove the yoke from your midst, the
pointing of the finger, and speaking
wickedness, and if you give yourself to the
hungry, and satisfy the desire of the afflicted,
then your light will rise in darkness,
and your gloom will become like midday.
And the Lord will continually guide you,
and satisfy your desire in scorched places,
and give strength to your bones; and you
will be like a watered garden, and like a
spring of water whose waters do not fail.
And those from among you will rebuild
the ancient ruins; you will raise up the
age-old foundations; and you will be called
the repairer of the breach, the restorer of the
streets in which to dwell.        *Isaiah 58:6-12*

Ideas and actions do have direct economic consequences.
Poverty doesn't "happen to people," at least not as adults. Those not
in poverty have a biblical and moral obligation both to use their
wealth to encourage the poor and to provide opportunity for
dignified self-help through labor. ALMIGHTY & SONS has a great
challenge and an incredible evangelistic opportunity in front of us.
To the poor, in both riches and wealth, we can lead them to prosperity
if we truly know how to get there ourselves: *"Who is the man who
fears the Lord? He will instruct him in the way he should choose. His
soul will abide in prosperity, and his descendants will inherit the land"*
(Ps. 25:12-13).

# CHAPTER NINE

# Justice and Equality Are Not the Same

*"Righteousness and justice are the foundation of Thy throne..."*    Psalm 89:14a

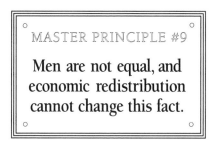

MASTER PRINCIPLE #9

**Men are not equal, and economic redistribution cannot change this fact.**

*E*very parent, business owner, manager, and leader faces the issue of human inequalities among those they lead, and has to decide what to do about them. Is everyone "equal?" Does the evidence of people's conduct support such a conclusion? What are their "rights," and what are their "responsibilities?" Do we treat everybody "equally," and if so, how? Out of these questions flow huge issues which affect us personally, managerially, legally, and nationally.

I know this: Line up everybody for a 50 yard dash; you'll see how "unequal" we are. Ditto for a math test. Ditto for drawing sketches. Ditto for people skills. It's the same for any comparison on any level between people. We aren't "equal." What we really want is "justice," so why do we keep calling it "equality"? Could there be an agenda here somewhere by some special group? Obviously. Whenever I hear "equality," I look for the hidden agenda.

Our age is being fed by the energy of the so-called "human rights movements," and most of the cultures in the Western world have become supremely preoccupied with the issues surrounding some of the questions we've just raised. Taxation policy, commercial law, quota systems, anti-discrimination, criminal proceedings, and foreign aid are just a few of the major social policies that are established out of how people and nations deal with these issues. We're dealing with questions that affect everyone's pocketbook, and everyone's freedom. In this book all we can do is point out some of scripture's relevant principles.

Believers must set out to disciple themselves, their families, their businesses, and their nations in accordance with those principles. But let it be known at the outset: The Bible doesn't teach that all men are equal, and no amount of social legislation or economic restructuring through tax policy can change this reality.

## Our True Equality Is In Terms of Our Responsibility to God

In what way can mankind then be said to be "equal"? The scripture comprehensively answers this question in multiple ways and verses: We are all "equal" before God to obey Him. Only in obedience are we equal. All men and woman are equally responsible before their Creator to walk by the particular light He has given to them, and will be judged accordingly. Indeed, the scripture holds all humans responsible before God for how each individual sought God in their own heart in response to His manifest presence in both nature and in His particular interventions which He brings into all our lives to call us to Himself.

Let's listen to Paul's dealing with this overall issue in Romans, chapter 1:18-22

> For the wrath of God is revealed from heaven against all ungodliness and unrighteousness of men, who suppress the truth in unrighteousness, because that which is known about God is evident within them; for God made it evident to them.

> For since the creation of the world His invisible attributes, His eternal power and divine nature, have been clearly seen, being understood through what has been made, so that they are without excuse.

> For even though they knew God, they did not honor Him as God, or give thanks; but they became futile in their speculations, and their foolish heart was darkened.

> Professing to be wise, they became fools.

Men have not been made equal, except in their responsibility to obey God. Man cannot restructure what he did not create. If man had created the Cosmos, he could restructure it; but how can he restructure what he at best only partially understands? God put within man the urge to take dominion, and he will attempt to restructure his world in any event. That leads us to the beginning of our next discussion.

## By What Standard Will Man Take Dominion over the Earth— His or God's?

As already noted, Adam was commanded to take "dominion" over the Earth.[1] God created the Cosmos and, as we saw in chapter one, the word "Cosmos" contains within it the concept of being cared for and tended. Deeply woven into the Cosmos and man himself is the need for man's discovery and stewardship of this universe. Paul saw this relationship between creation and man in Romans 8:17-22, and stated that the Cosmos is waiting for ALMIGHTY & SONS to repair, order, and liberate the very creation itself:

> For the anxious longing of the creation waits
> eagerly for the revealing of the sons of God.
> For the creation was subjected to futility, not of
> its own will, but because of Him who subjected
> it, in hope that the creation itself also will be set
> free from its slavery to corruption into the
> freedom of the glory of the children of God. For
> we know that the whole creation groans and
> suffers the pains of childbirth together until now.
> *Rom. 8:19-22*

The Cosmos was created expectant and anxious for man's stewardship, even though it was already "very good"[2] at the point of creation.

Man is not created for eternal retirement; he is created to steward God's Cosmos as an inspired landscape architect under the general

---

[1] Gen. 1:26-28
[2] Gen. 1:31

orders of God the Landowner. The creation is incomplete without man adding his creativity and innovation to its development. It is an eternally unfinished painting, glorious as it stands, but growing in splendor and meaning as the artist matures himself as he continues to work upon it. Man is not going back to Eden; rather, he is going forward to an unfinished canvas of unbelievable dimension and potential.

## We All Have the Desire to Change Things

This inherent urge to reshape and bring order is in all men, saved and unsaved alike. The fall didn't take God's imprint out of man. What it did was open up to man the idea that he should tend the Earth with his *own* set of plans, not the Owner's. Fallen man's rebellion is revealed by the fact that he objects to the Owner's blueprints for the creation and so has been stubbornly drafting his own plan, altering these counterfeit plans from culture to culture throughout history. These "blueprints" are called the "world system," which Satan energizes and oversees, hidden in the shadows, shrouded by man's arrogance and denial of Satan's control.[3]

The issue at hand, man's "equality" and the nature of "justice," is now contextualized in this drama. Fallen man attempts to decree both his own nature and how he *ought to be,* independent of how God *declares* him to be in the Bible. There are only two possibilities: man's own independent ideas for the Cosmos, or man's ideas as filtered through the nature of God and the laws and principles He has decreed. The Christian's choice is clear. In fact, to truly be a Christian we must stop interpreting reality with human philosophy, and submit to reality as God clearly declares it to be. In response to His reality we work in line with the truth. ALMIGHTY & SONS is a partnership based on a clear, eternal understanding of who is the Boss. It isn't man, and it isn't our ideas. Living in reality is living inside of God's perspective and God's laws.

---

[3] 2 Cor. 4:4

## Man's "Equality" Is Tyranny by Any Other Name

The heart of modern paganism is to attempt to make equal what God has made unique. For reasons we do not fully understand, beyond the obvious motive of envy, Satan hates the uniqueness God has put into His created beings, and Satan has transmitted that hatred into all fallen men and systems. God in His sovereign wisdom has chosen to give greater and lesser engiftments to men, and this is like waving a red cape in front of the sin of pride that snorts within our fallen breasts. Satan, and therefore his fallen world system, is totally hung up on "equality." God, on the other hand, is hung up on individuality or distinctiveness.

## "Equality" Is Dressed Up Envy

Two sections of scripture are particularly appropriate here. The first one, as might be expected, shows up in Satan's first entrance in Genesis. He projects his own preoccupation with equality onto God and attributes his own inner fears to the Almighty: "For God knows that in the day you eat from it your eyes will be opened, and you will be *like* God, knowing good and evil" (Gen. 3:5). *Being equal to or like God* is Satan's supreme passion. But "equality," driven by jealousy and pride, is never ultimately enough. "Equality" must give way to superiority, for its root is the desire to transcend. Again, Satan's heart and the heart of the "drive for equality" is revealed clearly in this scripture:

> How you have fallen from heaven, O star
> of the morning, son of the dawn! You have
> been cut down to the earth, you who have
> weakened the nations! But you said in your
> heart, I will ascend to heaven; I will raise
> my throne above the stars of God, and I will
> sit on the mount of assembly in the recesses
> of the north. I will ascend above the heights
> of the clouds; I will make myself like
> the Most High.             *Isa. 14:12-14*

This passion to be received as "equal," when coming into full bloom, changes faces. It starts with wanting to be "like," but it ends with wanting to be "better than." Small wonder that all "equality movements" generate tyranny and substitute a new tyrant of racism or sexism or classism over the old tyrant they most recently deposed. Please carefully think about this.

In fallen man's quest for "equality" he becomes what he declared himself to be against and reflects what he vowed to replace. Unable to achieve this dark transformation as an individual, he elicits the power of the state as his henchman. The state then becomes the champion of men's "rights," and "inequality" then becomes the nation's chief adversary. Politics becomes the machinery of greed and envy and pride. The state continually attacks each new-found enemy of public equality or political "correctness." God's distinctives are attacked; our mutual built-in needs for one another's strengths and weaknesses become increasingly buried under a sea of state and social propaganda. This shrill "moral voice" continues to demand "equality," and thus destroys the roots of humility and interdependence.

Freedom from tyranny or injustice cannot be achieved by one class of people oppressing another in the name of moral purity. Freedom comes when all men acknowledge their fallenness and their own special, and usually hidden prejudices, and fall on God's mercy to cleanse themselves and thus free their brother or sister. Any other method only makes the state more and more of a prejudiced bully enacting the prejudices of the regime currently in power.

### Pagan Equality and Tax Reform

The heart of modern paganism is to attempt to make equal what God has made unequal.

> Woe to those who call evil good, and good evil;
> who substitute darkness for light, and light for
> darkness; who substitute bitter for sweet, and
> sweet  for bitter! Woe to those who are wise in their
> own eyes, and clever in their own sight!...who

> justify the wicked for a bribe, and take away
> the rights of the ones who are in the right.
>
> *Isaiah 5:20-21, 23b*

Because the state has a socialist spirit and cloaks covetousness in the garb of compassion, it looks at different economic strata and concludes that if someone has more than someone else, he must have "ripped the other man off." So what is its solution to the problem? —tax and tax until the players are more equal.

God knows more about economics than all the economists. He taxes all His people at a flat rate—the tithe. It's ten percent of income after business expenses.[4] The tithe is a so-called "regressive tax." It violates all the modern laws of taxation, but it's a *just* tax because it's God's tax and weighs proportionately on everyone.

Civil government should demand no more than God does. *Its* tax policy should reflect *His*. If God charges a flat tax, civil government should. If God charges ten percent of increase, civil government should charge *no more*: no exemptions, no loopholes, no funny business—just like God's tax. Can you imagine a society where civil government played no tax games and took no more than 10% of our income? The release of capital creation and creativity would go through the roof all the way to the moon!

This message sells. But we need people to deliver it. That's you. That's your little army that you can raise up. This army will be made up of people who can explain that God is a covenant God and that inequalities don't just happen to people—they are the fruit of obedience and disobedience. This army will be made up of people who will serve sacrificially to deliver the poor from slavery under the welfare system. We need people who will invest their time and energy and love into those who need to learn the disciplines of true wealth: godly character, wise stewardship, and faithful work.

May God anoint you to carry the following message:

- To him who is faithful in managing what he has,
  God will give more.

---

[4] Num. 18:24-30; Deut. 14:22-28; 26:12

- God doesn't take from those who have in order to give to those who don't have.

- God takes from those who don't practice good stewardship to give to those who do.

- God doesn't reward disobedience and punish obedience.

- God rewards good management, but poor management has its own negative consequences.

God the Father is building ALMIGHTY & SONS, and He wants hundreds of millions of faithful partners to join Him.

## Understanding God's Justice

Life is not "fair," and only idealists, fools, or tyrants try to make it so. Life is a unique experience designed by God to make people grow up and let them become more and more of what they have chosen to be. Their lives are the soil from which their nature is revealed by their choices. In our fallen compassion we wish it were not so, and the apparent "cruelties" of unequal environments and events often go beyond our human abilities to comprehend how a God of love could permit it to be as it is, but He does. He expects us to trust Him, not to try to change the fundamental order of things. The following scripture clearly demonstrates Christ's concern for discovering and submitting Himself to the choices both God and man have made for themselves. Isaiah 42:1-3 states:

> Behold, My Servant, whom I uphold;
> My chosen one in whom My soul delights.
> I have put My Spirit upon Him;
> He will bring forth justice to the nations.
> He will not cry out or raise His voice,
> Nor make His voice heard in the street.
> A bruised reed He will not break,
> And a dimly burning wick
> He will not extinguish;
> He will faithfully bring forth justice.

Does this mean God is cruel, and that Christianity is heartless? Hardly. To negatively contrast the Bible (containing hundreds of verses calling for human intervention in suffering, poverty, injustice, and evil) with Buddhism, Taoism, Islam, or existentialism is an absurd joke. Indeed, the history of Christianity (its corruptions notwithstanding) is a study in the formation of hospitals, universities, orphanages, child-labor laws, and anti-slavery. Jesus is the foremost liberator of women and races ever to walk planet Earth.

Justice begins with the recognition of the uniqueness of all individuals before their Maker and one another. We look to God's Word for how that uniqueness is to be identified in each person and utilized for the needs of the many. Justice is God's idea (not man's) and transcends simple outward differences. A classic example of this transcendency of the obvious is found in Leviticus 19, often referred to as "all the law of God in one chapter":

> You shall do no injustice in judgment;
> you shall not be partial to the poor
> nor defer to the great, but you are to judge
> your neighbor fairly.          *Lev. 19:15*

God's common justice to all of us is summarized by Christ's supernaturally brilliant integration of the entire Law into His answer as to what is God's greatest commandment:

> "You shall love the Lord your God with all
> your heart, and with all your soul, and
> with all your mind." This is the great and
> foremost commandment. The second is like
> it, "You shall love your neighbor as yourself."
>                               *Matt. 22:37-39*

Man is to render to God what is due Him, and to his neighbor what is due him as well. And what is due to each of these? God's Word declares: "Man shall not live by bread alone, but on every word that proceeds out of the mouth of God."[5] To live justly, I must steward

---

[5]Matt. 4:4

things as scripture defines: my body; my natural and spiritual gifts; my relationships; my natural possessions; Christ's gospel; my salvation and the salvation of others; God-ordained authority; and my place in the spiritual work of both my generation and my nation. Justice is aligning ourselves with God's work rather than attempting to measure ourselves against each other, which Paul says is unwise.[6]

What then are our collective rights? They are outlined in God's Word. Let us not add to or subtract from any of them lest we release a curse upon mankind, as the closing words of the book of Revelation principally remind us.[7]

## The Role of the State As an Instrument of God's Justice

The civil government (one of the five God-ordained jurisdictions of government we shall study in the next chapter) is God's instrument of public protection. Romans chapter 13, verses 1 through 7, gives us the clearest New Testament picture of civil government's role in enforcing God's justice:

> Let every person be in subjection to the
> governing authorities. For there is no authority
> except from God, and those which exist are
> established by God. Therefore he who resists
> authority has opposed the ordinances of God;
> and they who have opposed will receive
> condemnation upon themselves. For rulers are
> not a cause of fear for good behavior, but for evil.
> Do you want to have no fear of authority? Do
> what is good, and you will have praise from the
> same; for it is a minister of God to you for good.
> But if you do what is evil, be afraid; for it does
> not bear the sword for nothing; for it is a
> minister of God, an avenger who brings wrath
> upon the one who practices evil. Wherefore it is
> necessary to be in subjection, not only because of

---

[6]  2 Cor. 10:12
[7]  Rev. 22:18-19

> wrath, but also for conscience sake. For because
> of this you also pay taxes, for rulers are servants
> of God, devoting themselves to this very thing.
> Render to all what is due them: tax to whom tax
> is due; custom to whom custom; fear to whom
> fear; honor to whom honor. *Rom. 13:1-7*

The whole of the text tells us three overarching truths: (1) we are to honor civil government and those administering it as God's servants, (2) we are to recognize that it is established to carry the sword against evil, and (3) we are to pay the taxes due it to carry out these reactive duties, as we shall shortly see. It is very clear from this text that civil government is called to be a guardian of God's order, not an architect for a new one. It is to be reactive in nature rather than pro-active. Civil government should not seek to establish any program, but rather to reinforce the one that God has already set forth in His Word. We are to pray that its work will be benign, a background operation, so that the foreground of man's salvation and dominion can be worked out in peace and order:

> First of all, then, I urge that entreaties and prayers,
> petitions and thanksgivings, be made on behalf of all
> men, for kings and all who are in authority, in order
> that we may lead a tranquil and quiet life in all
> godliness and dignity. This is good and acceptable in
> the sight of God our Savior, who desires all men to be
> saved and to come to the knowledge of the truth.
>
> *1 Tim. 2:1-4*

Nowhere in the Old or New Testament is the state urged to become an economic "equalizer," transferring wealth from the productive private sector into the non-capital producing public sector. The state is *not* called to minimize risk (as we discussed in chapter seven); reduce fair competition; promote bureaucracy; centralize power away from local states, provinces, or regions; or transfer wealth from one family to another. "Equality" is the propaganda used to publicly justify most of these sinful practices.

It is the task of ALMIGHTY & SONS to conduct their own lives and enterprises based on *justice,* not *equality.* Out of the authenticity of that witness, we can then press the outer world to obey Christ's standards as well.[8] If we do not ferret out "equality" from amongst ourselves as Christians, we will remain divided and full of envy, working against each other, and all working against the goals of our Master. Say it loud, children of the Owner.

*"Let justice roll down like waters..."*    Amos 5:24

---

[8] Matt. 28:18-20

# CHAPTER TEN

# Godly Government Produces Peace and Productivity

*"There will be no end to the increase of His government or of peace..."*  Isaiah 9:7

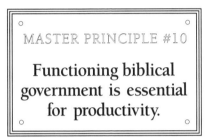

MASTER PRINCIPLE #10

**Functioning biblical government is essential for productivity.**

To study good government we must study God's government; His government is the standard and pattern for us unless we choose to go our own way. God (the Father, Son, and Holy Spirit) is one God in three Persons Who is and governs as One. The Trinity is not only a Self-revealed fact; it is a community within Himself. As the ancients say, "God is within Himself a sweet society."

The Trinity is the ultimate revelation of government, mutual service, the concept of division of labor, and the complete model of unity. All successful organizations should pattern their governing principles after God, unless they think that they can come up with a better idea. Without the life of the Trinity, man would have no exact model for government. To study God's government is to study both how to make things work properly, and also to study our future, for indeed our future is to become joined with God's government in ways we cannot yet understand.[1]

God the Father has determined that God the Son will embody the fullness of God,[2] and all power will reside in Him. In Colossians 1:13-18 Paul states the following:

---

[1] John 17:21
[2] Col. 1:19

> For He delivered us from the domain of darkness,
> and transferred us to the kingdom of His beloved
> Son, in whom we have redemption, the forgiveness
> of sins. And He is the image of the invisible God,
> the first-born of all creation. For by Him all things
> were created, both in the heavens and on earth,
> visible and invisible, whether thrones or dominions
> or rulers or authorities—all things have been created
> by Him and for Him. And He is before all things, and
> in Him all things hold together. He is also head of the
> body, the church; and He is the beginning, the first-
> born from the dead; so that He Himself might come
> to have first place in everything.

It is clear that Christ is both the center of all government and the One in whom all power resides. Whatever power any man or God-ordained institution of government holds, it holds because Christ has given them a part of His authority to exercise within their appointed sphere. Because the Godhead has divisions of labor and jurisdictions within Itself,[3] man and the created order must follow suit.[4] In other words, what we see God doing, we should seek to follow.

All government is united in Christ; lesser governments are limited and bound together in service and submission. This is the pattern for all businesses, nations, and families. Someone, or some group, is the ultimate executive, and all lesser governments must follow the directives of the head, and interrelate to each other as the head so directs. When this pattern is operating biblically, order, creativity, and productivity are the results. When it isn't, the results are confusion, dependency, and poverty. This isn't the wisdom of Harvard Business School; it's basic Bible government course 1A. Good managers understand these truths and build their organizations accordingly. They know that clear biblical government is essential for productivity.

---

[3] John 5:22; 15:1; 16:7-16
[4] Gen. 1:26

## God Is the Source of Sound Government and All Human Rights

As we have already noted, all human government is bequeathed by Christ to man and held in trust for Him. A man can do nothing, as Christ reminded Pilate,[5] unless God permits him to do so, and all lesser government must answer to Christ as the Supreme Government. Similarly, all human rights are derived from Him. As you know, the Declaration of Independence, upon which the governing Constitution of the United States rests, begins with the assertion that, "We hold these truths to be self-evident, that all men are endowed by their Creator with certain inalienable rights..." Human rights come from God to man, rather than man to man.

Because of the Fall, man's ability to govern himself became subject to corruption and needed redemption in Christ. Human government, dispensed by and patterned after the Trinity, was established in a kind of check-and-balance pattern, foreseeing the potential for corruption which unified power brings to fallen man. Lord Acton's statement that "Power corrupts and absolute power corrupts absolutely" is true for fallen man, though obviously not true for Christ since He has ultimate power, and it hasn't corrupted Him.

As I pointed out in my first book, *Winning the Battle For the Minds of Men,*[6] Christ has separated His divinely ordered institutions of human government into five basic spheres. All human government, with both its rights and responsibilities, are presented in the scriptures according to these five jurisdictions: (1) self-government of individuals; (2) the government of the family; (3) ecclesiastic government; (4) commercial government or voluntary associations; and (5) civil government. Each has specific duties and powers, and all are to function in mutual submission to God and serve each other. All of them have limited power, and all of them have rights which are God-ordained. Without understanding these biblical principles, believers cannot properly function as a part of God's Kingdom government. Without this understanding believers will not correctly perceive organizational

---

[5] John 19:11
[6] Pages 18-27

unity, will not function properly as citizens of their nation, and will not be able to properly lead either their family or their professional life. The following diagram, taken from *Winning the Battle for the Minds of Men* (pg. 20)[7] should prove helpful:

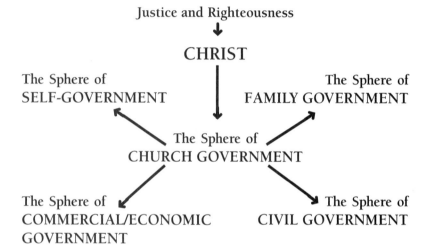

**THE FIVE SPHERES of HUMAN GOVERNMENT**

## GOD'S THRONE
*Psalm 89:4*

**Justice and Righteousness**
↓
## CHRIST

The Sphere of
**SELF-GOVERNMENT**

The Sphere of
**FAMILY GOVERNMENT**

The Sphere of
**CHURCH GOVERNMENT**

The Sphere of
**COMMERCIAL/ECONOMIC GOVERNMENT**

The Sphere of
**CIVIL GOVERNMENT**

To better explain this diagram here are some excerpts from the book:

> Notice that the Church is at the center of this diagram, Christ is over the Church, and God's throne of justice and righteousness presides. The Church is to be the priestly, teaching, and prophetic voice to the world. Its responsibility is to correctly interpret the Word of God to all the forms of government. Its job is to hold that Word up to all other institutions, including itself, as a plumb line for human conduct. (pg. 20)

---

[7] Dennis Peacocke, *Winning the Battle for the Minds of Men*, Santa Rosa, Strategic Christian Services, 1987

A Christian philosophy of government in each of these five spheres consists of the ability to make sure that power is properly held and balanced proportionately for each governing institution. The Bible provides us with these guidelines.

Tyranny is not some dark figure out of the night, leaping into the midst of society. Tyranny is abuse of power. Tyranny results from the improper accumulation of power in one institution or sphere. The whole modern culture is moving deeper and deeper into tyranny under the misguided principle of centralization. The anti-God forces are continually transferring more and more power to civil government, in effect castrating our individual freedom, our families, our churches, and our economy. The centralization of power into the state is the most dangerous trend in the world today. (pg. 21)

If Christ is not reigning, then either the individual, the family, the Church, the commercial realm, or the state will rise up as a false point of human focus. Men will always deify one or another aspect of the creation. Carnal man cannot avoid worshipping the created rather than the Creator. Even the Church, strange as it seems, can be exalted to tyrannical power in a Christian's life, becoming out of balance with both the Lord and the other institutions of human society. (pg. 22)

When the *individual* becomes the focus of human government we have anarchy; when the *family* becomes the centering focus we have tribalism; when the *ecclesiastic order* becomes the center, we have religious wars; when the *commercial order* becomes unbalanced, we have cut-throat monopolies or some form of fascism; and when the *civil government* becomes the power center, we have statism. When any sphere is out of place or balance, we have the loss of liberty, the increase of tyranny, and the suppression of the human element of God's Cosmos.

Since this is not a book directed at understanding government, per se, we must move on. Suffice it to say, to us as Christian business professionals, commerce does not operate in a vacuum. Understanding these basic laws of biblical structure and government is not only essential in terms of running our own lives and organizations, but it is also essential in correctly responding to what is going on around us as our political/economic structures continue to go deeper into crisis. This book isn't written to make you rich; it is written to add to your wealth and serve you in preparing yourself to better rule in a world undergoing major change.

## Why Is Our Philosophy of Government So Important?

Our philosophy of government either stimulates or retards human creativity and productivity. The systems of thought by which we organize people and things are like the software by which we program the hardware of the modern computer. The utilization of the full capacity of the hardware is limited by the directions it receives from the program. That is exactly how the "programming" of our philosophy of governments works; if the philosophy is weak, then the maximum capacity of the organization goes unused.

The heart of a government rests in its view of power. Do those in control have "power over" others, or do they have "responsibility for" others? We talked about this in chapter five, but it requires another look from this added vantage. As we saw in the passage in Luke 22:24-27, true authority in God's Kingdom is of a servant nature. When we approach leadership responsibility from a "power over" perspective, besides opening ourselves up to pride, we begin to put those under us in a mode where their creativity button switches "off." Their primary concern becomes the *fear of authority* rather than *the accomplishment of the task at hand.* Fear of man (or failure) is non-productive and self-imprisoning, whereas faith (that I can do the job and my leaders are here to help me do it) releases enormous energy. Those of you who are familiar with the situation in Eastern Europe know exactly what I mean when I say that this is a classic example of the long-lasting negative effects of humanistic "power over" authority: killing creativity and the faith to produce. I cannot over-emphasize this point: The spiritual atmosphere your leader produces in the work place is the single greatest key to productivity and creativity.

The "power over" philosophy of government proceeds from a kind of Darwinian, evolutionary mind-set, wherein survival of the fittest justifies power, rather than power being justified by its capacity to draw life out of those related to it. Government that rests in raw strength or intrigue produces death, whereas government that rests in eager-ness to release potential, produces life. Love is grounded in the reality that every person has intrinsic value because they are fashioned in the image of God. Evolution, on the other hand, gives us a view of life where people are in fact "evolved slime-balls," and have no intrinsic value beyond what we choose to give them. Christian leaders must see that every person's dignity must be enhanced and protected in God, and their gifts revealed and developed. This is the driving force behind truly Christian organizations.

Hierarchy, as we saw in the last chapter, is a fact of God's creation. We are not all equal. Even though the members of the Godhead are ontologically "equal," the members of the Godhead relate under Father's hierarchical authority as a universal example to us. Hierarchy is essential for order, protection, and the development of humility. A hierarchy, in order to lead in a godly fashion, must endeavor to develop each person under its authority to their greatest potential. In essence, the leaders must get "under" their people and push them up to success. Can you imagine the productive revolution that could take place if believers in marketplaces began to organize and lead in this fashion? Instead of the adversarial model of labor/management antagonism, which is the world system's management style, there would be a true government of service. To what degree believers will experience this on the Earth prior to Christ's return is unclear, but one thing we know for sure: ALMIGHTY & SONS' eternal govern-mental relationships will operate with hierarchy and love perfectly balanced. All of us need to start increasing our skills in this kind of leadership now.

## Breakdowns in Government Will Spread

We have said that godly government produces order, initiative, and productivity, whereas ungodly government produces confusion, dependency, and poverty. No better example of this truth exists than what has been happening in the demise of the public education system in America. Once a world leader, our educational system has degenerated (in many places) into a true "blackboard jungle" where fear, rebellion, and confusion have all but destroyed an atmosphere where true learning is possible. The teachers and school authorities have lost their right to teach because the "rights" of some students to act like jerks have somehow become greater than the rights of the other students to learn. The parents have lost control, drunk with the permissive wine of secular psychology. As a result, the unresolved governmental problems of the *home* are pushed onto the *school,* which in turn ends up pushing them onto *society,* the *marketplace,* and the *criminal courts.* What isn't solved at home goes public in some form. A breakdown in human government never stays fully contained.

As we see government collapsing around us, know this: It cannot collapse for very long economically. For this reason economic evangelism is perfectly fitted to impact all cultures: Economic survival is the one common need for which man will come into submission. When the government of the marketplace functions in the biblical pattern, which it must to survive, its example will force a mandate toward the redemption of the other spheres of government which have become so corrupt and out of balance.

Speaking foolishly, who cares if self-government is lax? Who cares if the family unit is defined as thirteen bisexuals, four transvestites, and a horse living together? Who will really notice if the Church splits into eighteen million denominations? We can even put up with lousy civil government for a long time. But what we *cannot have* is the marketplace falling apart, because there goes our ability to work and provide for ourselves! In the modern world, which sphere of government do you think people care about most? Obviously, economics, and that is precisely why it must become, and will become, a key focus for Christian revival and world change.

## "That Government Which Governs Least, Governs Best"
### *Abraham Lincoln*

Modern political theory, which was my academic field of study, is undergirded by the Kantian-Hegelian notion that the state is "God walking on the earth." The state and the process of civil government have become the politics of salvation for the masses. This philosophy has claimed that the state will solve our problems. As a result of such a philosophy of government, the responsibility for change in the modern secular state rests at the *top*, rather than down at the bottom with the people. That is the unspoken assumption of modern society: Change comes from the top down. However, out there in the real world there is a growing army of dissidents who are rejecting that nonsense. They know change comes from the bottom up, through *people who seize control* over their problems and destiny.

## The Worship of Democracy Is a False Hope

The "will of the people" and "power to the people" are slogans of the modern global society, with few exceptions. Democracy has become our new idol of worship, especially since the demise of the Soviet Empire. Democracy is being touted as the answer to the world's problems. But pure democracy has always been the nightmare of most political scientists and historians, for they know the mob-rule chaos it has always produced in history. The French Revolution is exhibit "A." "Democracy" can become the cruelest form of tyranny, and indeed, it never lasts. It always is replaced by either cultural collapse or cultural strong-arm tyrants. In contrast, biblical government is in the form of a republic,[8] where wise leaders are chosen by the people to rule on their behalf, and to some degree, beyond their basic interests. It is for this reason that Calvin and others of the Reformers said that civil government was the highest ministry calling on Earth for any believer, since it is from this office of public service that a whole society is pastored and governed. Where are the churches today who aspire

---

[8] Ex. 18:13-26; Num. 11:16,29; Acts 6:2-6

to, and are training future government leaders? Where are the churches who are self-consciously training future C.E.O.'s in biblical management skills? This is what the Church must do if we are to really change things. We ought to put our energy into training, not complaining!

The government that governs most effectively and productively in the marketplace or city is largely unseen and appears in strength only when it is needed. Otherwise, it tends to overshadow and weaken the resolve of those within that organization who need to take responsibility for their own tasks. Once this is understood, those in leadership positions will focus on imparting the long-term vision for their organization to others who are working there. The goal would be to help each individual make that vision "his own," and to help him see the vital role he plays in the process. The scriptures give us exactly this kind of manual, if we have "eyes to see" it. As we learn God's governing patterns, we are experiencing Almighty's vision and making it "ours."

Clear biblical government is essential for productivity. Our philosophy of government is critical. What is your philosophy of government? Is it clearly defined to those over whom you have influence or responsibility at home, work, church, or in society? If it isn't clear to you, by what criteria are you governing and by what specific principles? What are you doing to enhance people's productivity, increase their skill levels, and enable them to thrive in an atmosphere that recognizes mistakes and corrects them, but focuses primarily on developing potential? All of us must stand in these kinds of self-examining questions.

These aren't new ideas. The issue is not their novelty, but rather their *practice*. ALMIGHTY & SONS is an organization of disciples, and that means those who practice truth.[9] May we become truth practicers who understand the relationship between good government and creative productivity. Why should the business schools be doing the Church's equipping for us and on their secular terms? They shouldn't. Since the vast majority of our congregations work in

---

[9] Heb. 5:14; 12:11; Phil. 4:9; Prov. 6:20-28

the marketplace, we ought to be equipping them to do so effectively. Come on, "ALMIGHTY" brethren, look beyond the Church's four walls; that is where the action is.

And may I also suggest that we substantially add to our church Sunday school curriculums and pulpit themes? We need those forums to instruct our believers how to practically function—in biblical fashion—in the real world instead of inspiring them to "feel good" with sermons that usually begin to fade by the end of the church parking lot. If believers are going to be real, we have to get real. And remember, this is a "pastor" who is saying these things.

# CHAPTER ELEVEN

# The Essential Threefold Cords that Will Lead to Your Success

*"And when they did not find them, they dragged Jason and some brethren to the rulers of the city, crying out, 'These who have turned the world upside down have come here too.'"*                                                    Acts. 17.6 (KJV)

> ○                                    ○
> ## MASTER PRINCIPLE #11
> **Christians must live as disciples, renew their minds, and come together in unity to execute God's plan for the nations.**
> ○                                    ○

All of the principles that we have discussed so far will remain relatively powerless unless we consistently and self-consciously apply them. In other words, knowledge of truth only has power when applied properly, consistently, and with explanation to those who are being affected by its application. To multiply truth, we must be able to teach others how to both understand and use it as well. Unless we do this, that truth remains only available to ourselves and therefore we cannot expect to change our immediate environment, let alone a nation.

In order to teach, we must discover what we know, and also what we don't know. This is a process because it is only through teaching that my students' questions and different learning styles reveal to me my ability (or inability) to explain to them clearly how something really works. With this I whole-heartedly concur: The fastest way to learn is to teach.

All of this is laying a foundation for this simple premise: True Christianity is about information that leads to transformation. Christ's supreme earmark upon those people or situations that He touched was this: After He left, people were different. While this book is about basic and foundational biblical truths of economics and business practice, I am passionately committed to something beyond simple teaching. I want to see Christ glorified in this world through His people, and glorified specifically through the practices of capital creation and empowered people. To see this accomplished, we must all make three basic practices a part of our lifestyle:

1. We must become disciplined learners (disciples) so that we can master God's truths, for our own sakes and for the sakes of those we are called to teach.

2. We must build a truly biblical Christian worldview, which begins by rooting out the deceptions the world system has carefully planted in our hearts and minds.

3. We must seek out others of like mind in order to network and build with them for the purpose of spreading and multiplying God's truths in the marketplace and out into the extended culture and decision-making centers.

The remainder of this most critical chapter, then, is about how to take personal responsibility in our own lives to build a delivery system for the truths and concepts to which we have said, "Amen."

## SQUARE ONE
### Only Disciples Change the World: Are You Living Like One?

> And Jesus came up and spoke to them, saying, "All authority has been given to me in heaven and on earth. Go therefore and make disciples of all the nations, baptizing them in the name of the Father and the Son and the Holy Spirit, teaching them to observe all that I commanded you; and lo, I am with you always, even to the end of the age."                    *Matt. 28:18-10*

A disciple is a disciplined learner, one on the journey toward mastering those truths which have truly captured their heart. While Christ plainly called all "Christians" to be and make disciples, large numbers of us aren't living as such. The name "Christian," a term applied to us by mere men, is only used three times in the scriptures. "Disciple(s)" is used over 250 times. Folks, there is a clue here, I think!

Discipleship, as a lifestyle (not a "program"), is wonderfully suited to the marketplace world because the feedback systems of results are so quickly and easily revealed. The laws of sowing and reaping act more quickly in business than in any other realm of coordinated human activity. Business ideas and actions usually have a rapid turn-around time, quickly showing up in tangible "bottom line" results. Because of this, seeking to discover, apply, and master God's concepts in the business world carries with it enormous short-run possibilities for the building up of our faith that God's Word really works. Out from this will flow evangelism, remarkable success stories, and a whole new perspective on the place and value of marketplace ministries and issues. But, this is all based on the delivery system God allows us to build for His truths. If He calls for disciples, then disciples are what He will use to carry the heart of His message's transforming power.

This is not a book on "discipleship," but let me describe what I consider to be the critical elements of discipleship we must embody to effectively bring our lives to the point of being change-agents for Christ in the marketplace or anywhere else:

- **A captured heart**—Disciples have been captured on a heart level by what they see as truth, beauty, justice, or "sense" in some set of ideas or skills, usually as displayed by another person. (Examples: sports, the arts, intellectual truths, money-making skills, spiritual skills, mechanical arts, etc. All of these arenas carry elements of truth, skill, art, and reward that capture hearts.)

- **A standard of truth**—Disciples must have a standard of truth, ethics, and excellence to measure their progress against without "lowering the bar." For believers, this is obviously the scriptures.

- **A motivational power source**—Disciples must have a compelling vision that empowers them to train, as well as handle hardships, discouragement, and all the other obstacles that stand between a novice and their quest to master what they aspire to be and know. Humanly speaking, this is called the power of a committed will. Believers need *both* a committed will and the power of God's Holy Spirit.

* **A source of instruction and correction**—Self-teaching only goes so far. True disciples need coaches, teachers, and encouragers who will "speak the truth in love" (Eph. 4:15), bringing correction when it is essential to further their learning and progress. Genuine disciples must be humble enough to be corrected and clear enough on what the truth really is to not be set "off course" by false teachers or unfounded opinions.

* **A "B" side vision**—Many "normal Christians" seem primarily to live life on the "A" side of personal motivation. What I mean by this is that their primary motivation and scope of life centers around their own welfare and those closest to them. A "B" side player is motivated by Christ to be used to play at such a level that their life can be used to affect many others. Their quest for mastery is driven by a vision of glorifying God and His Kingdom at the very real expense of their own lives and personal convenience. Their lives are lives in training and their standards of "success" are Jesus, Paul, and all the other men and women of the Bible whose lives were given for the sake of others. Christians go to heaven; "B" side Christians change the Earth on the way.

Without learning how to live life as a disciple, the measure of change we should expect from our lives (in terms of our influence on others in the marketplace or anywhere else) will likely be very modest. In contrast, hearts on fire will take the ALMIGHTY & SONS franchise throughout the earth and into eternity. Truth that is neither modeled nor incarnated is abstract, and therefore relatively useless.

## SQUARE TWO
### Building a Christian Worldview: Have You Started the Task?

> And do not be conformed to this world, but
> be transformed by the renewing of your mind,

that you may prove what the will of God is,
that which is good and acceptable and perfect.
*Romans 12:2*

For though we walk in the flesh, we do not
war according to the flesh, for the weapons of
our warfare are not of the flesh, but divinely
powerful for the destruction of fortresses.
*2 Corinthians 10:3-5*

...but speaking the truth in love, we are to
grow up in all aspects into Him, who is the
head, even Christ.     *Ephesians 4:15*

As the above scriptures clearly point out, the reordering of our minds is an essential task. It is not an easy one. Only genuine disciples will start up this mountain because it is a difficult task and often hard work. The world system has seen to that. After all, "Pharaoh's" system of education has very effectively brainwashed most of us, pouring into our minds a different moral, intellectual, and spiritual universe than the one God created (and in which we actually live). Beyond that, "Pharaoh" constantly reinforces that false universe as he influences the spending of billions of dollars in the media, arts, entertainment industry, newspapers, and magazines.

I was once proud of my advanced education at Berkeley until one day I saw what had truly happened. Pharaoh taught me history, economics, psychology, literature, science, and all the rest. About 25 years ago, I began the arduous task of yielding back to God a "renewed mind." I am still at it. If you saw my library of Christian books, you would believe me.

If per chance you think you "escaped" Pharaoh by going to a more moderate university or college than Berkeley, you are deceived, my friend. Having home-schooled all our children before we sent them out to battle, I know something about what I'm saying. What they were exposed to, even in Christian education, had many areas where world-system assumptions were covered over with well-intentioned Christian ethics. I am an unapologetic pre-suppositionalist. That means I want to know the origin and assumptions behind ideas or "truths" before I buy them. A Christian view of all truth requires the rigors of such examination. Anything less may still get us to heaven, by God's grace, but it won't be a strong enough antidote to the world system's falsehoods to change the Earth.

This book was written (and is still a work in process) of my journey to think biblically in the realm of economics, business, and social policy. With God's help and the wise input of others, my search in the scriptures for these principles and how to apply them has been a wonderful and, at times, exasperating journey. Perhaps one of the hardest parts has been watching the media, and listening to social commentators, "business people," "economists," and politicians wax eloquent on these kinds of issues, knowing that neither they nor the audience was prepared to think deeply enough or biblically enough to bring our economic and social policies into some semblance of true reality. Please hear my heart: We don't simply need Christian marketplace ministries "validated" as spiritual, or Christians making tons of money by applying God's laws; we need Christians with a biblical worldview who will reeducate millions of people, one sphere of influence at a time. My first book, *Winning the Battle for the Minds of Men*, was driven by that motivation. It too is a work in process.

We need some form of local, regional, national, and international educational study groups for Christians called to the marketplace who really want to develop a functioning worldview which will serve them and their ministries. At Strategic Christian Services, we have developed the Business Leadership School,[1] which is beginning to fill that gap, but we all need much, much more. When I hear the politicians arguing about certain business-related tax cuts "benefitting the rich," I want to pull out my hair. Obviously, they and many of the American people do not have the foggiest idea how investment capital starts business enterprises and creates jobs! We desperately need Christians who have a biblical worldview as it relates to the marketplace. We believers must do something about this, and it should begin in our local churches and in the businesses Christians own or manage.

---

[1] Please see "Additional Resources" at the back of this book for more information.

## SQUARE THREE
## Working Together Strategically to Execute God's Plan for the Nations: Will You Start Where You Have Influence?

I once asked a seminar audience: How do you eat an elephant? Amidst laughter and consternation, I gave them my answer: one bite at a time. That, friend, is how the world is changed. One bite at a time. God moves from concentric circle to concentric circle, ever larger in size and influence. I'm not asking people to join an organization; I'm asking them to join a movement. That "movement" is defined as bringing God's truth to bear, strategically and for the long haul, within your particular sphere of influence. Remember, God's plan to extend His rule over the whole earth began with only two people in a garden.

I am sure that you are attempting to apply all that you know where you have influence in general, and where you work in particular (at least when you're "on your game"). What we all need is to do it more consistently, more self-consciously, and more effectively. Consistency has to do with our habits and clearing our heads enough to get out of the tyranny of the immediate and urgent, and into the reality of how to "build our way into God's destiny for us" on a daily basis. To do so "self-consciously" means that we know what we are doing, why we are doing it, and how to know if it is being effective. While there is much we could say about living consistently and self-consciously, for the sake of our discussion, I prefer to focus on how to "build more effectively."

The game of change is a game of leverage. The smart players find people, ideas, organizations, or resources that can be leveraged to multiply (not just add) a desired change. A well-placed fulcrum, with a long enough and strong enough lever, could, as Aristotle is reputed to have said, "Lift the world." So it is in bringing change; we need to find the right leverage points.

Can I tell you where those leverage points are in your family, church, business, or any other organization? They are the true leaders or true influencers. Some of them may not even be officially recognized as leaders, but they actually are. Your task is to help them capture the organization's legitimate vision. This is where exponential growth truly begins in an organization.

How do we know this? Is it the stuff of Harvard M.B.A. programs? Not really. As we Christian disciples ought to expect, it is found throughout the scriptures. God's Word is the source of our foundational truths. Jesus and the way He sought out the twelve disciples, taught and trained them, and then released them into their ministry with His heart is "Exhibit A" to the quest for modeled leverage.

From a leadership perspective, your task is to find those who hear your (God-given) vision. Who are they? They are the ones who ask your advice and input and put it into practice. It really is that simple. It's the people that do what we suggest who are signaling to us that they are capable of being trained to be a leader and therefore a leverage point person for the vision. It's not about position. The real question is: Are the people in those positions the right people? The "right people" need three things to be qualified to be there:

1.  **Honesty**—that is, they give you their "inner conversation," not just the outer one designed to please people.

2.  **Competency**—that is, they have the quest for mastery which fits their calling. That quest is even more important than their current knowledge base. Current knowledge bases top out; the quest for mastery doesn't. If they're not seeking mastery, they're not yet carrying a disciple's heart.

3.  **The capacity to be trained**—that is, the wonderful quality of having the humility to learn from another, and the character to jump into someone else's dream without envy or the need to control it.

Once you start to build this way, you're on the way.

The game then becomes focusing your prime time on these leverage-point people and fending off everything else that can be fended off. And we all know that most things, and many people, demand quick and immediate attention. They form the tyranny of the urgent, but not the stuff of the strategic. A successful organization builds this way, and its leaders and managers are trained to look for new leverage point people and to build upon them. This is how employees become proprietors, and proprietors become points of leverage. Leverage point organizations become healthy organizations, and healthy people and organizations seek to relate to larger spheres beyond themselves. Now I am ready to sketch out our final point in this strategic chapter.

That which is truly healthy will always seek to interface with larger healthy units. As a wise man I knew once said, "This is the principle of internal integrity and external integration." God's universe is filled with this truth: Unity, and the ability to work together, comes out of smaller healthy units fitting together to form larger healthy units. Look at the human body. It is a perfect example of this truth. Cells fit into common cell groups; cell groups fit into organs; organs fit into systems; and systems fit into the leadership of the head. What doesn't fit is either isolated in the lymph nodes, eliminated, or cancerous. Healthy people and organizations integrate; unhealthy ones don't.

Obviously, when we are talking about integration in the business world, we are not necessarily talking about mergers or independent businesses looking for larger companies to join or buy them out. Neither are we talking about vertical integration or the effectiveness of economics of scale.

What I am saying is that healthy individuals fit into healthy departments, which fit into healthy divisions, which fit into healthy organizations. Whether the enterprise is large or small, the ability for smaller units to seek to add their strength to the larger units, which are a part of the same organization, is an essential sign of both personal and organizational health.

Individuals, departments, or projects which do not properly integrate are the cause of not only great concern to the leaders but substantial losses in both productivity and profitability.

The better our personal ability to fit into the plans of the larger organization, the keener will be our own ability to discern between those who have this skill and those who don't.

This law works in families, churches, businesses, and nations. Our goal is to become healthy so that we can fit into God's plan for His whole body—one life, one family, one church, one business, one industry at a time. Am I thinking too big or too unrealistically? Reread Christ's prayer to the Father in John seventeen and tell me that I am. Those who can hear the "ALMIGHTY & SONS" sound can hear what I hear and see what I see. *Doing Business God's Way* is about the three essentials in this chapter:

- Become a disciplined learner
- Retrain your mind biblically
- Seek to strategically network as you build through leverage-point people

These three building skills are essential in order to put legs to the truths we have discussed—truths that will otherwise remain only in the world of "abstract" or "religious" concepts.

# CHAPTER TWELVE

# A Call to True Radicals

*And those from among you will rebuild the ancient ruins; You will raise up the age-old foundations; and you will be called the repairer of the breach, the restorer of the streets in which to dwell.*                                        Isaiah 58:12

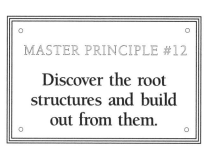

MASTER PRINCIPLE #12

**Discover the root structures and build out from them.**

## "Radical" Doesn't Mean What You Think

The world has always been changed by true radicals. They are the men and women who perceived the root issues of their times and pressed others to deal with the implications. Most men live dealing only with symptoms; true radicals are drawn to those unseen forces that underlie and shape the visual and transitory. Radicals deal with principles, while politicians and the like deal with sentiments, opinions, and achieving consensus.

"Radical" is a socially derogatory word. Few people concerned with effecting change want to be called one. This is a classic case of the general culture's ignorance of our English language, for the word "radical" actually means nearly the exact opposite of what most people believe it means. The word comes from the Latin root "radix" which literally means "root" or "root-issue." True radicals are not wild-eyed, long-haired, establishment-hating iconoclasts. Quite the contrary, true radicals lean far more back to the past and to their roots, for their passion is not the new and the progressive, but the old and the eternal. Radicals may indeed be spectacularly innovative, but their innovation is to be found in applying *root-structure truths* in fresh ways in order to bring a better future to pass.

Radicals reaffirm stabilizing truths, while false dreamers and power-seekers simply don the garb of radicalism. True Christian radicals are concerned with building on eternal foundations and with the One called "the Ancient of Days."[1]

John the Baptist was a radical, not because of his strange appearance and unusual lifestyle, but rather because of the reactionary message he embodied. He called men and women to radical love, and radical moral and ethical consistency. Radicals can and have also worn expensive clothing rather than camel hair suits or semi-nakedness, for radicalism is far more of a primordial sound than a primordial appearance. Radicals and radical messages grab our hearts and help us rediscover that we have roots amidst the dulling, numbing banality of the superficial, upon which society's "leaders" float and focus. Radicals inspire people to remember the ancient boundaries of time-proven truth. Faddists mimic the rebel; history pivots upon the radical.

God is looking for Christian men and women who will dare to be and live radically. This message, that Christian business professionals will take a significant place of leadership in the coming years, and that God is building a cosmic enterprise, will be viewed as "radical" by some. Indeed it is such a message. My burden in Christ is to find the men and women who want to change the absurdity of what is, so as to rediscover and rebuild what has been lost:

> Then they will rebuild the ancient ruins, they
> will raise up the former devastations, and they
> will repair the ruined cities, the desolations of
> many generations.        *Isaiah 61:4*

### Radicals Build on the Foundations of God's Laws and Principles

The world, and sadly, some of the Church, would have us to believe that laws are relative and that few ultimate foundations really exist. For these folks, the Old Testament has been replaced by the New, rather than the New being *built upon* the Old. They believe science can and has altered the nature of man; that history can teach us little (because we have evolved and established complex new relationships

---

[1] Dan. 7:9

with each other and our current environment); and that we are somehow unique. They believe that nothing is "fixed" (contrary to fundamentalist doctrine); that to hold onto past root structures is to become trapped in past errors; and that legal systems must "evolve" and keep step with our new technologies, liberated values, and mores. Anchors or foundations are just things that ground you and destroy your freedom. So they say.

But they have not fooled me with their arguments. They claim that their new laws are morally and religiously "neutral." I know they lie. No law is neutral, for all law proceeds from one's values about good and evil and what should and should not be. That is the stuff of religion. They especially have wanted to lie about the laws of the marketplace. They have tried to tell us that managing people and things in the real world is "carnal"; that the Church should have no part of it. They have said the marketplace is a lessor thing and possibly a manifestation of Satan's world authority. The godly are to live from it but not waste their time trying to change it. How can that be, since we spend more time dealing with the economic necessity of provision for our lives than any other activity?

My response to the secular economists, politicians, and would-be philosophers regarding ALMIGHTY'S economic laws and programs is this: Because only the Bible reveals the truth about God, man, and economics, only Bible-believing, Bible-obeying Christians can produce and sustain economic prosperity and justice. To do it, we must reeducate generations of people raised up under the lies of secular economics, and we must *model* the economics of ALMIGHTY & SONS, if we want others to follow. We must restore godly men to the leadership of our communities by training them in the Church! Again, we love to complain, but we seldom train.

The world would like us to believe that economics is a value-free science unrelated to morality. That is a lie; a lie that stands at the root of the economic troubles of our time. It is, in fact, the same basic lie Satan told Eve in the Garden: "Never mind what God says; reject His law; define your own rules; be your own God."

Some say: "Economics and science are about hard facts, not about values and religious philosophy." Right.

How do we know economics isn't a value-free science? First, no science is value free. All science values knowledge above ignorance, truth above falsehood, and honesty above dishonesty. These are moral values, and they cannot be justified by empirical science alone. They can be justified only by appealing to the Fountain of all morality, God.

Second, economics is the law of the household. (The word comes from *oikos* [house] and *nomos* [law].) It is not mere physical law; it is moral law, as we have already seen.

All law assumes a lawgiver. The laws of economics must come either from finite and fallen man or from the infinite and perfect God. As Christians, we believe they come from God. It is no accident that the founder of modern economics, Adam Smith, was a *moral philosopher* trained for the Presbyterian ministry. He was thoroughly familiar with Thomas Aquinas, Samuel Pufendort, and other Christian writers who preceded him in economics, and he considered economics the application of moral philosophy to market relationships.

Third, economics values profit over loss, but that preference cannot be justified by empirical (utilitarian) methods alone. It can only be justified by appealing to God, the Source of all profit, Who made everything from nothing by the Word of His power and made man in His image to follow in His footsteps.

In every way, economic foundations in God are as real and necessary as moral foundations. As we've discussed, successful economic and management laws must be built on a godly foundation: the laws of service and empowerment, the spheres of jurisdiction, the truth that God pays for what He orders, and more. Those laws are as real as the laws which prohibit theft, murder, adultery, or the like. A wholistic God has not created a fragmented or compartmentalized universe. His laws are the foundational fabric, i.e., the "roots," that tie it all together and undergird what happens to us as we obey these laws or reject them.

## "Basics" Are the Key

The issue then comes down to finding the basics and sticking to them. By "basics" I mean the fundamental building truths that underlie any successful action, system, or enterprise. Wise business professionals must discover the foundations of what they or their businesses are called to do and stick to those foundations. Basics are everything. The more complex an organization becomes, the stronger the commitment to basic law, basic purpose, and basic execution must be. Diversity unhinged from basics is cancer. As we read God's Word through the eyes of our calling, its application comes alive. Do you see the building principles I see in this verse?

> And He said to them, "Therefore every scribe
> who has become a disciple of the kingdom of
> heaven is like a head of a household, who brings
> forth out of his treasure things new and old."
>
> *Matthew 13:52*

Among other things, we see the cantilever principle: You can only build *out into the new* to the degree that what you are building is anchored in the old. True growth is "out from" and "related to."

What I have attempted in this study, in an introductory fashion, is to help us recognize the way we view God's relationship to the private sector, the private sector's relationship to the world, and the Church's relationship to both. Each is a basic relationship, a foundational relationship, and each must become a radical relationship.

## On the Nature of Revival and Revolution

Revolution is based on the notion that if you change external relationships you will change the nature of man. Indeed, you may change his behavior, but his innards remain the same. History's latest example of this truth is Marxism. It came; it is going; and nothing was changed about the foundations of man. All it did was oppress and kill multiple millions of human beings and press the West into a massive diversion of resources into the defense industry. But for all the revolutionaries' dreams and rhetoric, five-year plans, and revisions of history, in the ultimate scope of things it was descriptively captured by Shakespeare: "A tale told by an idiot, full of sound and fury but in the end, signifying nothing of great importance."[2]

A revival, on the other hand, presupposes internal change: To have a born-again world we must have born-again men and women. I cannot bring change to what I cannot see clearly, and I cannot see clearly God's standards and Kingdom until I am born again.[3] Without His Kingdom laws as a measuring rod, I have no objective tools to repair or cast down what the world system has built.

Having attempted to introduce the basic concepts of biblical economics and management in this book, I remind us once again of some of the principles shared in chapter one. They form a biblical point of departure for true economic and social revival:

### Six Essential Laws for Rebuilding a Culture

1. **Personal Initiative:** All true freedom begins in self-government under God.

2. **Healthy Families:** The family unit is the basic building block of a healthy society.

3. **Effective Churches:** The local church is the primary equipping center for effective Christian service.

4. **Private Property:** The stewardship of private property is essential to personal and societal maturity.

5. **Problem Solving:** Rebuilding a nation begins with rebuilding local communities.

6. **Strategic Thinking:** Wars are won with ideas.

The action plans that we recommend and have been seeking to help Christian leaders implement (both in the United States and abroad) are based upon these general principles and the other principles in

---

[2] The Tempest
[3] John 3:3-5

this book. These principles lead to a strategy that rebuilds the foundations of our culture. In the economic realm, our strategy must begin by calling the *elders of the city back to their city gates.* Once working relationships are established, the elders can then begin to strategize together regarding how they can truly serve God's will for their community as they apply selective resources as a unified force. This is the goal of what are called, "City Action Councils."

As a result of man's revolution against God, especially economically, here is what we are already beginning to see throughout the nations:

### Institutional Break-Up

> And His voice shook the earth then, but now
> He has promised, saying, "Yet once more I will
> shake not only the earth, but also the heaven."
> And this expression, "Yet once more," denotes
> the removing of those things which can be
> shaken, as of created things, in order that those
> things which cannot be shaken may remain.
> Therefore, since we receive a kingdom which
> cannot be shaken, let us show gratitude, by
> which we may offer to God an acceptable service
> with reverence and awe.                *Heb. 12:26-28*

> Translation: "There's a whole lot of shakin'
> going on" and coming.

### The Defunding of the Public Sector

The defunding of the public sector through revenue disintegration is rapidly taking place. God is not mocked. As the economic and moral consequences of abortion, debt, fiat money, the welfare state, and other evils pile up, the West will reap what it has sown. We will continue to experience increasing bankruptcy, particularly in the public sector. The public revenue tax base will dry up. Federal government will increasingly shift economic responsibility beneath it until all government is as bankrupt as the federal government. The state will no longer be able to shield people from the consequences of their sin. Families will be forced to care for their own because nobody else will be able to. Federal, state, county, and city government will begin to economically crack.

Our strategy, the vision of ALMIGHTY & SONS, is to prepare the Church to be a safety net on a grassroots, community level; to rebuild families; and to bring Christians out of debt so that when the time comes, they will be prepared to serve and enable. The collapse need not hit everyone. The plagues God sent on Egypt didn't touch Goshen, where God's people lived. God is covenantally faithful to the righteous in the midst of judgment.

The collapse of the international monetary system will happen. How soon? We don't know. The system still has considerable resiliency in it and will withstand some more body blows, but eventually the fictions on which it is built will be revealed as a foundation of sand.

We believe God will enable His Church to put its own economic house in order and be prepared to rescue people from destruction before He sends the judgment, just as He gave Noah time to build the ark before the flood. If I didn't believe that, I wouldn't bother writing this book. We have to believe there's time for the Church to obey. God gave Joseph time to build granaries before the famine struck. That's the kind of God we serve.

## Preparing for Judgment

What must we do? We must reeducate and mobilize spiritual leaders. Renewal and change begin with leaders. We must go to the leaders in the Church, in the economic community, and in the business community. We must work in our communities to set up City Action Councils. These councils must work to unite Christian leaders in business, the media, local government, community service, activist groups, and churches to seek God's will for the community.

In council, the forces of the private sector, equipped with biblical truth and empowered by the Holy Spirit, can seek biblical solutions to the community's problems and work with the civil leaders (who are God's deacons [Rom. 13:1-4]), to build real safety nets in every community. Then we can string those nets together from community to community so that they can communicate across the nation, sharing what works, and learning from each other's successes and failures. That's our strategy in a nutshell.

We obviously believe in electing Christians to all levels of government. However, simply electing Christians into public office will not "change everything." The system has to be changed from the bottom up, not from the top down. The *ideas* that drive our culture must change and so must the citizens' levels of participation and political competency. That is God's way. God wants to start with small things well done. That's why *localism is the key.*

A holy God enforces His laws. Our country is under judgment. We, His people, are under judgment for how we apply His truth to our communities and our nation.

"Is judgment coming?" you ask. Open your eyes and look around! If judgment isn't having the schools able to send your daughter out to have an abortion without your knowledge, what is it? But the Bible says, in Isaiah 26:9 (KJV), "...when thy judgments are in the earth, the inhabitants of the world will learn righteousness."

When everything that can be shaken is shaken, what cannot be shaken will emerge from the rubble. That gives us hope. We're not the prophets of doom and gloom. Our message is that God's judgments bring righteousness!

Looking forward to what will be born through God's judgments excites me. You and I are privileged to be here in an hour of unimaginable historic change. The God who works through history is calling us to take part in that change. He even wants to use us to bring it forth.

Kingdom economics is not one of several options for economic prosperity; it's the *only* option at all! Millions of people, even non-Christians, will respond to this message. Up until now, most never knew God was the God of the whole creation. They thought He was only the God of what you eat and drink and whom you sleep with. That is why they have looked at our religion as nonsense. It was too small and too unrelated to the larger real world. But when we share the principles of a covenant-making and covenant-keeping God, the unbelievers will say, "Why didn't you tell me this before? We thought Jesus was a Sunday school figure who only cared about our sexual ethics."

The measure of our ability to bring change to any situation is the strength of our biblically-based vision and heart-based passion for that vision to come to pass. While this book is the fruit of many years of study, teaching, and reflection, its basic truths are not complicated, however deep their implications. If you can understand in one reading all that is here, something is surely wrong with me for having taken so long to absorb these truths myself!

Therefore, here is what I am asking you to consider doing to help facilitate the transforming power Christ has placed in you to help bring about the needed changes we are advocating:

1. Reread this book.

2. Conceptually memorize the twelve principles. If you haven't committed them to easy memory, you will have difficulty recognizing situations where they are in play in real life.

3. Deepen your time with God in reflection; the fast pace of life "traffics" our soul and doesn't allow sufficient time to act truly strategically through spiritual principles rather than simple business pragmatism.

4. Look for opportunities to share these ideas; they pop up every day if we are interacting with God's Spirit and listening with the ear of a disciple.

5. Consider having discussion times in your local church with your business colleagues (this book has an already prepared accompanying course), or releasing your employees to share in an "at work" education time.

## It's "Show Time" Brothers and Sisters!

The business community is ready to support a flat income tax and the abolition of land tax, corporate tax, and inheritance tax. Parents and even many educators are ready to support defunding public education and raising up competitive private education in its place. The poor and those who care about them are ready to support the overhaul and reformation of the welfare system. Police, lawyers, and judges are ready to support the reform of the criminal justice system and a return to justice based on the Constitution. Are you ready to take the message to them? Are you a spiritual radical? Are you born again enough to see the Kingdom of God?

May God help us to respond to His call by saying, "I must rise up and build. I must take the truth into the private sector and my home, and wherever else I have an influence. I must live out these principles where I work and evangelize with them. Help me, Lord, to go to the private sector and give them the life-transforming message of ALMIGHTY & SONS."

The enemy will never expect us to engage the real world with practical truths; that's our secret weapon. We believe God owns it all, and that He is in the business of tightening His market share until only His will is being done and His Kingdom has come on the showroom of Earth as it is being done in the management offices of Heaven.

If you simply read this book without beginning to apply it, our journey together has been less than successful. Change requires action and practice. May you be provoked and inspired to both: All our futures are mutually resting on each other's responses. And ALMIGHTY AND SONS continues to expand forever and ever...

## About GoStrategic

Founded in 1979 by Dennis Peacocke who serves as President, GoStrategic is a prophetic ministry committed to training and equipping leaders of every cultural sphere in discipling nations to transform the world. The Business Leadership School (**www.businessleadershipschool.org**) and Strategic Life Training (**www.strategiclifetraining.com**) schools educate Christians through online training supported by Facilitators and real-time group interaction. In addition, GoStrategic produces educational products, hosts events, networks, and consults. Our ministry headquarters are based in Santa Rosa, California, with affiliates and schools in Mexico, Central and South America, Europe, Asia, Australia and New Zealand.

GoStrategic equips believers to be leaders in the communities where they live, work, and serve. We specialize in bridging the gap between spiritual truth and the practical implementation of those truths in confronting real-world problems. With over three decades of experience educating, modeling, and connecting like-minded individuals, we have seen first-hand the fruit of Christians applying Biblical principles to the most complex challenges. It is our sincere hope that the services we provide result in thousands of communities transformed as believers step in to rebuild, repair, and restore our world. To learn more, please visit the GoStrategic website at **www.gostrategic.org.**

800-700-0605
707-578-7700
info@gostrategic.org
www.gostrategic.org

# BUSINESS LEADERSHIP SCHOOL

GoStrategic's Business Leadership School began in 1996 with the mission of training businesspersons how to build businesses God's way. The school is a two-year correspondence course based on biblical principles of economics and business practice, and the inherent concept that deeper learning follows effective service to others. BLS provides a sharply-defined perspective for how biblical truth impacts marketplace thinking and practice, and how it produces transformation in participants' lives and businesses.

We help open the Scriptures to you to "see" the universal building patterns and how to apply these life-changing and capital-producing truths to your life and to those you lead and influence.

**Results of the Business Leadership School:**

**Vision:** A sharply defined perspective for how biblical truth impacts marketplace thinking and practice.

**Foundations:** Critical ideas foundational to a trajectory in manifesting God's Kingdom in the marketplace.

**Connection:** A process that helps connect participants with other resources in a larger context to foster change and promote transformation in personal life, family, business, and community.

**Facilitation:** Trained Facilitators provide direction to participants, encouraging and helping them examine their thoughts, attitudes, and practices in light of the principles presented in the course.

BLS currently operates in the US, Mexico, Canada, Europe, New Zealand, Asia, and Central America.

**To learn more, please visit our website:**
## www.businessleadershipschool.org

# Marketplace Audio Series by Dennis Peacocke

### The Freedom Series

In this unique audio series, Dennis shows how we can use our marketplace skills and our love for God to provide a better future for our family and help change our nation. CD/MP3, 8-Part Audio Series with Workbook.

### The Management Series

Based on the book, *Doing Business God's Way,* this series includes the teachings: *Four Basic Business Skills, We Grow Up Caring for People & Things,* and *How to Discern Whom & What You Can Trust.* CD/MP3, 3-Part Audio Series with Workbook.

### Worldview for the Marketplace

This series will engage your interest and affirm your calling as you are presented with 12 Master Principles that undergird a Christ-centered approach to your labors in the marketplace. Receive a biblical foundation for marketplace ministry, learn to live and work strategically, and build a biblical view of managing people. CD/MP3, 15-Part Audio Series with Workbook.

Available at **www.gostrategic.org/store**

# More Audio Series by Dennis Peacocke

### Let's Talk

This series on communication skills provides breakthrough material for healthier relationships. It is designed to capture the interest of believers and unbelievers alike to discover the power and life of applying God's principles to relationships. Learn how to build or rebuild, strengthen, and maintain a "bridge of trust." CD/MP3, 7-Part Audio Series with Workbook.

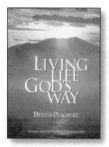

### Living Life God's Way

This popular series offers a comprehensive, proven plan with daily steps to energize and motivate you to stay awake to the possibilities that God brings your way while avoiding potential pitfalls. Find guidance on the path to personal transformation and learn to truly move beyond the hurts of life. CD/MP3, 8-Part Audio Series with Workbook.

### Producing Commitment

This series is a classic teaching for leaders wanting to instill vision and inspire action. Dennis deals with vital topics such as, *Calling People Who will Change the World, Producing a Sense of Destiny,* and *The Heroism of a Life Poured Out.* CD/MP3, 7-Part Audio Series with Workbook.

Available at **www.gostrategic.org/store**

## Other Books by Dennis Peacocke

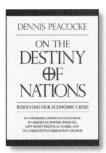

### On the Destiny of Nations: Resolving Our Economic Crisis

Dennis Peacocke's latest book provides an informed Christian challenge to absurd economic policies, left-right political games, and a frequently irrelevant church. Paperback, 185 pages.

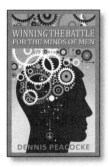

### Winning the Battle for the Minds of Men

Christianity once turned the world upside down, but today it is considered irrelevant. How did this happen? Why did the 20th century Church retreat into what Dennis Peacocke calls, the "Christian Ghetto?" In this book Dennis provides us with answers, exposes the lies that are crippling the Church, and reveals how we can recapture the original vision and power for discipling all nations. Paperback, 180 pages.

### The Emperor Has No Clothes

A compilation of 17 years of *Bottom Line* commentaries yields bountiful fruit of insights into popular culture and personal responsibility. Thematic chapters address subjects from "The Challenge of Personal Growth" to "The Quest for Reality in Politics." A great introduction to Kingdom thinking. Paperback, 192 pages.

Available at **www.gostrategic.org/store**